AF263649

THE RIME OF THE ASIAN HIGHWAY

A 70s overland journey to India remembered in verse

The Rime of
The Asian Highway

A 70s overland journey to India remembered in verse

John Webster

John Webster Publications
Oxford

First published in Great Britain in 2022
by John Webster Publications
© John Webster 2022

The moral right of John Webster
to be identified as the author of this work
 has been asserted in accordance with the
Copyright, Designs and Patents Act of 1988.

All rights reserved. No part of this publication
may be reproduced, stored in a retrieval system,
or transmitted in any form or by any means,
electronic, mechanical, photocopying, recording,
or otherwise, without the prior permission of both
the copyright owner and the above publisher
of this book.

ISBN 978-1-0683328-38

ACKNOWLEDGEMENTS

With thanks to Supriti Isaac for proofreading and canny suggestions, Asiya Zargar of Indus Experience for giving 'Asian Highway' a presence on YouTube, Anthony Swift for friendship and encouragement, John Carey for generosity and goodwill, Premila and Jonathan for suggestions and perspectives, and to all those who developed the 'fourteener' verse form used for storytelling since who knows when. Every effort has been made to trace the origin of the photograph of the Grand Trunk Road on the cover; more information would be welcomed about this image so reminiscent of many of our days on the 'Asian Highway'.

For Premila, Jonathan,
and the return of
travelling days

Contents

Beginnings

I don't know how it happened, but it just fell into rhyme,
The first steps of a journey that had long been on my mind.
For me, highly significant in terms of my life's course,
And with a set of memories that lingered on in force.

And then I saw that oh-so-famed Charge of the Light Brigade,
Called 'elegant doggerel' by some wit on comment page.
And that was a relief! I thought 'Well I'll settle for that',
Rather than with new style thrill the commentariat.

And go with Wordsworth's 'emotions recalled in solitude',
With a bit of Byron's epic style without being too rude.
So with Wordsworth, Byron, Tennyson – guys, can I go wrong?
I hope that in the end you'll like my unpretentious song.

For nowadays this odyssey has gone down history's pan,
You might well get through Turkey but be hostage in Iran;
Afghanistan, Pakistan (maybe) are simply no-go zones,
But you can trace this journey from the comfort of your home.

One thing that I must mention now is about my friend Ann,
The first girlfriend I ever had whose courage sparked our plan.
She, just like me, half Scottish was, and half English as well,
She liked the fact that I had maps – in company we fell.

And she skipped with pleasure when I came to her Scottish home,
And as I'll say we settled then into a travelling mode:
Intense at times, but we all have our personalities,
And with the strain of travelling, they flutter in the breeze.

The trouble is, I really can't narrate this through her eyes,
Just assume that we were fine unless told otherwise.
We could rough it, *had* to rough it, with expectations small,
So we rubbed along just fine as the world we did explore.

And we were open to answers outside our upbringing,
To chew rice slowly – that enlightenment would surely bring?
An era of false starts, dead ends, yet progress still unfurled,
We saw ourselves as truly finding patterns for the world.

So now please let me offer you our journey told in song,
I think better than a novel, for that would be too long.
I also hope that you'll enjoy the pleasure of the rhymes,
I'll do my best and hope that they don't seem too strained at times.

So that's my introduction – now we must get underway,
After a night with Brixton friends, we set out one fine day.
With our packs upon our backs and new boots upon our feet,
We stuck our thumbs out by the road and waited for release.

Into the unknown

By the road in Blackheath, only 19 years old,
With autumn leaves a-gathering, four thousand miles to go!
It was not that we were wanting to locate the mystic East,
Rather it was on experience that we desired to feast.

It had started with a question, 'What shall we do with this?'
There was some surplus money – and her answer came back quick:
'Why don't we go to India? That's always been my goal' –
And from that very instant we assumed a traveller's role.

So there we were in Blackheath, with four thousand miles to go,
Both anxious but excited and becalmed beside the road.
As we would learn repeatedly the first lift of the day,
Could seem to take forever – when would we get underway?

And yet it happened: we were off, and France was soon behind,
From Mont Blanc's approaching tunnel we saw lorries crawl in line.
Then down the autostrada fine for southern Italy,
A ferry from Otranto's pier would see us on to Greece.

A setback here – the ferry had packed up just recently,
For memory's sake we picked a fig and dipped into the sea.
Then got back in time to Brindisi to catch the ferry there,
Sleeping on the deck, I think, and breathing pure sea air.

Then waking in the morning to see Albania's shore,
Bathed in a gorgeous pastel light that filled us both with awe!
We reached Igoumenitsa, got a lift before too long,
We moved on up through mountain roads that twisted on and on.

Little owls stared out from olive groves, then we were in the plain,
Approaching Mount Olympus and then still on again.
Passing Thessaloniki as the night began to fall,
We crashed out on a stony hill and slept there till the dawn.

And then we woke to find a tortoise crawling happily,
And a shepherd from Australia – an aborigine.
I should really say 'indigenous' (but that would spoil the rhyme);
We shared a fellow feeling as we'd all left much behind.

We got some breakfast somehow, though I don't remember where,
But ouzo with the coffee clearly was the standard fare.
We got out on the road again with morning packs so light,
We now knew they'd be heavy at the coming of the night.

Our last hours in our Europe home we sensed a change of state:
A house, Alexandropoulis, eyes painted on the gate.
Then land that flattened steadily as we headed out of Greece,
A river at the border post that heralded the East.

So now we were in Turkey, and the land grew sparse and spare,
Two engineers, vacationing, thought we'd be company there.
Their four-wheel drive Land Rover – an impressive set of wheels,
That duelled with passing buses and would try a march to steal.

They lamented they'd run through their cash, back in Switzerland,
So close to things exotic now – but little left in hand.
As if to rub it in about their thwarted aim to rove,
We found a seashore campsite in a pretty hazel grove.

They took us on to Istanbul, we saw the city wall,
So massive, though unable to prevent the city's fall.
It loomed up as we drove right in under the eastern gate,
Then dropped in city centre as the afternoon grew late.

Now what to do? We had a guide, a xeroxed paper thing,
That predated the Rough and Lonely books that now are king.
The pudding shops were where to go and orient with friends,
So soon we were a-hanging out, discovering travellers' trends.

Food simmered in the shopfronts and the jewellers blazed with light,
Arcaded markets showed a cornucopia of sights.
The blue mosque was a marvel with its vast and tranquil space,
There in its culture resting, one of beauty, danger, grace.

As night fell army vehicles prowled through the darkened streets,
But in our cheap and dingy rooms we had a safe retreat;
And there we put our feet up, with a jug of Turkish wine,
Reflecting we were one third there – just six day's journey-time.

And so, to Asia…

Next day we took the ferryboat and crossed the Bosphorus sound,
Out of Europe into Asia, the moment seemed profound.
We looked back over Istanbul: its minarets and domes
Stood against a pale blue sky as the wake behind us foamed.

We found the right bus station and quietly waited there,
Of nearby warlike preparations we were unaware.
Now in territory new and described as Middle East,
Apprehension and excitement in my own case at least.

Then, when we were underway, another change we found –
In Europe, nearly everywhere, Man's signs are all around.
Now as the bumping bus moved on, through mountain valleys vast,
Humankind dwindled to nothing, its power overcast.

And the driver's habit was, on a long descending slope,
To just turn off the engine and allow the thing to coast.
I guess to save some petrol he would let the journey ride,
A serene silence descended as we did the downwards glide.

We still ground on, then on and on, and day turned into night,
Yes, there were three long days of this – before we saw the sight
We'd paid the ticket price for, the Iranian border post,
The country that was destined as our new and short-term host.

We were then just through Erzurum and in the neighbourhood,
Was the mountain in the Bible where Noah's ark had stood.
Where it came to rest or boarded from, I'm afraid I do not know,
But we saw it in the distance – its summit topped with snow.

But I digress, this is no good, we've got to get along,
To try the reader's patience here would be completely wrong.
After all we've only just begun and there's so far to go,
So let's resume the narrative and not let the story slow.

Ok, so we were in Iran, the country of the Shah,
Whose modernistic impulses at that border post we saw:
New and western décor and those shiny drinks machines,
Border guards immaculate with uniforms so clean.

Another stretch of purgatory and we were in Tehran,
Dumped by the company's offices long hours before the dawn.
A grimy alcove our refuge, we sat upon our packs,
While a shirtless man's contortions strange, saw his body racked.

Tehran, a bustling city, with countless impatient cars,
Beyond the mountains with their snowlines, neither near or far.
The streets a male-only preserve, with dark and intense eyes,
We bought a ticket out of there and stayed a single night.

It must have been at this time that began that desperate war,
That shook the world's complacency, its oil needs underscored;
Known since then as Yom Kippur, fought over Israel,
We headed east to Meshed and still thinking all was well.

On east again, but to Taibad the lorry had to go,
We were stood there in the desert both elated and alone;
A sign read 'The Asian Highway', and a red sun slipped from sight,
A solitary shepherd gave us shelter for the night.

Spending Afghan time

Next day the Afghan border post loomed up out of the sand,
Our visas were in order – we were in Afghanistan!
A driver of a small bus offered free rides to Herat,
We settled back into our seats just thinking that was that…

Except that on the desert road it soon ground to a halt –
A high price was demanded and no way could we default!
A 'deceitful Oriental' as the Iron Duke would say,
We didn't care too much at all as we were on our way.

Opposite our hotel room a blacksmith's hammer chimed,
Coming in and out of consciousness with the passing of the time.
That evening a gentle gathering in golden candlelight,
With luscious fruit and company that gave us all delight.

The light upon the hotel's wall revealed all was handmade,
The shadows on the surfaces with that light interplayed.
We all felt dislocation from the system of the west,
But in our new surroundings, all tension we'd divest.

We were tempted in that mood to praise and idealise,
Those Afghan men who strode the streets seemed to be filled with pride.
The little boys who called 'baksheesh' - 'my friend I have hotel',
On the surface it was wonderland as far as we could tell…

Except we'd found our knapsacks had been clearly patted down,
By the Afghans on the bus top when we'd travelled into town!
We travelled light, no cameras, but a razor went, how weird!
The universe, I thought, was wanting me to grow a beard.

We saw the mosque in Herat with transcendent turquoise wall,
We heard the muezzin's summons – the faithful for to call;
The same mindset we'd witnessed on the bus across Iran,
When it would stop, and all got out to pray there in the sand.

There was a burgeoning tourist scene that catered to us lot,
With bakeries and craft outlets and scarf and carpet shops.
Invited in, out of the sun, to an exotic room,
The shop's owner poured us mint tea among the carpets strewn.

He told us then of Yom Kippur, it seemed so distant here,
And of the coup in his own land, earlier in the year.
The king had abdicated, he had just thrown in the towel,
And his successor was OK he said, a not unpleasant guy.

So that was maybe why the streets were seeming so relaxed,
With every one adjusting to those not unpleasant facts.
Outside the sunlight slanted and the light of noon declined,
He cared not if we purchased: we were passing Afghan time.

So that was the Herat that we saw, then on to Kandahar,
A shiny road three fifty miles with desert stretching far;
In the distance jagged mountains, sometimes a valley green,
At night the stars and moonlight were the clearest that I'd seen.

A hotel with braying donkey hitched to a nearby tree,
We soon got awful tummies there, reputedly from ghee.
But someone told me later of the city's water source –
Loaded with impurities and undoubtedly the cause.

In Scotland, where we'd started out, we'd found our travelling way,
Of hitchhiking and camping out and with that we would stay.
Whether it was wise to stick with that now in Afghanistan,
Dear reader, you'll discover, and before we leave this land.

But we wanted to explore outside and set off with our packs,
Soon finding ourselves blundering round, rescued by some chap!
In his fine grove of pomegranates as the hoopoes called,
We spent a tranquil afternoon within his garden walls.

And in the night the villagers took us in so readily,
It was not so much that it was love but just of their duty.
So if you offered thanks to them, that would be brushed aside,
Ascetic men in turbans white, both hard and dignified.

In a long and whitewashed room we ate, with those men so fine,
With mutton, bread and yogurt, and all sitting there in line.
No women to be seen at all, completely out of sight,
And there, in deep Afghanistan, we spent a peaceful night.

Then next day in the morning, men in uniform came round,
Set us on the road at whose end Kandahar was found.
Our same hotel regaining, we hung out and played it cool,
After days of readjustment we set out for Kabul.

And there we found a great hotel the Friends Hotel by name,
We could camp out in its garden, other travellers did the same.
Round the corner, Chicken Street, the home of much exchange,
With all of us young westerners whose tastes were ascertained.

The post, back to our families, took just a week from here,
So off went letters and our progress we tried to make clear.
In the garden, with its birds and under the blue sky,
Our songs were sung, our poems done, and Afghan time went by.

Contentment led to boredom; a decision then was made,
To see Paghman, a beauty spot, where local rich folk played.
An Aussie recommended it, and in his camper van,
We set off one late afternoon through rugged stone-strewn land.

And yes, it did get beautiful, and by a running stream,
We set up camp, climbed the hill, watched the light amid the trees;
We cooked a meal back at the tent and then our friend was gone…
The darkness had descended full and we were quite alone.

We moved later up the valley – and on a terrace flat,
Found ourselves a sheltered spot and at a modest height.
At night the wolves were howling we both slept fully dressed,
Some boys warned us of bandits, but we thought that we knew best.

Until one night warm in the tent we heard a rustling noise,
Then voices getting closer and we realised those boys
Had oh-so-wisely warned us and we'd been arrogant –
We gathered money, passports and retreated in the tent!

And then a bullet head poked in with knife in his right hand.
I held his wrist, the blade was blunt, I pinned it to the ground.
In these situations, my philosophy is restraint –
I talked at him in soothing tones his intents to negate.

Now, he'd got in by opening the tent's horizontal zip;
The tassel for the vertical, I reached out for and gripped
To be prepared for escalation, just by instinct this,
At crisis point to throw it wide and feel the night air's kiss.

Then he rushed in, and we rushed out, and found ourselves outside,
On that ledge a-standing by the embers of the fire.
The tent there and his accomplice still standing by its side,
Down the slope we jumped as one and ran as for our lives!

We got back to the village and knocked on a tavern door,
Its owner simply sheltered us with no fuss as before:
He turfed his son out of his bed and there we stayed the night,
Returning to our waylaid tent, in morning's early light.

'Experience will tell you what you can and cannot do',
So said the Incredible String Band and yes, that sure is true;
Yet back in our Kabul hotel we pitched our tent once more,
Sensing in its compound space that we were quite secure.

So out to stroll in Kabul's streets under the bright blue sky,
With all its sights and sounds and the baker's strawberry pie;
The cafés with their mint tea and with giant chess boards new,
The crusted pots of yogurt and the fresh-baked naan breads too.

Our next step was to hit the road to reach Jalalabad.
After Paghman you'll be thinking probably we were quite mad,
But it was easier for us somehow and we sensed it was ok,
A well-off guy then stopped for us, and we were on our way.

Our packs he covered cautiously, so they were out of sight,
We got on well – a charming man – he put us up that night
At his place in Jalalabad where we were glad to stay,
And all was well … the only thing was when I went away

For a nocturnal loo break … well then I returned to see
Him over by our bedside – he recoiled immediately;
But after that it all was fine, we slept until the day,
And thanking him we loaded up and set out on our way.

Ahead the Khyber Pass of fame that snaked its rugged way
Up through an epic landscape where the Pashtun tribe holds sway:
Its summit, with the border post, that signalled a new land,
On a brightly painted lorry, we set off for Pakistan.

You can see the pictures for yourself, on the internet,
The road uniquely wild and so, once there, you can't forget;
The ruined forts, the mountains sheer, the sense of history,
The knowledge that the law is made in your vicinity.

We benefitted from a code of welcome there impressed,
The lorry cab, a home for us, where we would be the guests.
For driver and assistant, we would brighten up the day,
They were our protectors and would see us on our way.

It is said, for geo-strategists, all parts of our fair world,
Can be deemed of vital import in their strategic terms,
But Landi Kotal for definite which tops the Khyber way,
Deserves that title fair and square, and still does to this day.

On a historic trading route it's witnessed armies strong,
Pass on their way to India or to do the Afghans down.
The British Empire made its mark though quite late in the day,
Who knows what's now transpiring, with the Taliban in play?

Pakistan illuminations

From border post in Pakistan, we rolled on down the hill,
And found in crowded Peshawar a nice whitewashed hotel;
With rooms around a courtyard and with music blasting out,
They had just one Beatles single, namely, 'You Can't do That'.

That evening, with light fading fast, the birds arose as one,
Setting off for who knows where, in flight from the setting sun;
Peshawar was a frontier town, not everything was right,
We heard shots in the street outside one Peshawari night.

The food in all the restaurants was cooked with spices wild:
A real change from Afghanistan, the spices there were mild!
A mighty piece of ginger in the final bite we'd find,
Red-faced and perspiring a whole chilli we declined.

We had India in our sights, we should have caught the train,
And yet I'm glad we went by road for as I shall explain…
Travelling close to land and people can bring its own return,
And soon there was an incident from which I later learned.

For as we set off, packs on back, to find the edge of town,
A smartly dressed man then appeared, politely flagged us down;
'Would we like some chai'? he asked – 'Well sure that would be good',
He found for us a little shop and chai appeared – with food.

And he produced a wad of notes and turned his face to me,
A proposition then was made which I realised gradually
Was not altogether decent, in fact, quite the opposite:
He hoped that I would take the cash and authorise a tryst

Between him and my partner who was sitting there bemused,
He didn't even look at her or conceive she could refuse!
The meet it grew in import as events and years went by,
A real and lived experience which to issues grave applied.

So later, when the penny dropped, I began to understand,
A woman was the property, the chattel of the man.
He'd thought her at my sole command, for me to use at will,
And earn myself some rupees too if that would give a thrill.

So now, as we are on the brink of leaving Muslim lands,
Let me put my thoughts in order and try to understand
The true nature of this mindset and how it operates,
And works in our society and to the world relates.

For everyone is mixed up now and trying to get on,
To understand how cultures work: that surely can't be wrong.
So if I take some time and unashamedly digress,
I hope that you'll be patient and not think of me the less.

Now in most situations we found we could travel free,
An assault on her would violate what was 'my property'.
So that gentleman of Pakistan had done 'the correct thing',
And when I declined the offer, well he took it on the chin.

The trouble comes when cultures connect uneasily,
With that sexual code imported and with no attempt to ease
Its workings in the western world where other codes hold sway,
Freer and more liberal where love can find its way.

I'm thinking here of what we've seen in cities and in towns,
And how this must be the mindset, that drives the 'grooming gangs':
Where no man is in the picture there need be no control,
As was seen so very clearly some years back in Cologne.

And sadly too, the women can be quite aligned with this,
Their boys 'are blameless, it's the West, the girls just ask for it';
Someone told of desperate mothers hoping that they'd intercede,
The Pakistani Centre's door was slammed – no trace of 'ruth or rede'.

But a shameful racist legacy means we can't see this plain.
So, from fear of being in its wake, the Law itself abstained.
Forgotten was the motto – 'The Children of the Poor Defend',
A craven outlook took its place – 'Watch Out We Don't Offend'.

And this was then the vacuum that the grooming gangs enjoyed:
To act out with impunity and work their countless ploys,
To prey on the weak and vulnerable who needed care and love,
They gamed with them unhindered by officials credulous.

Now UK judges often say 'You treated her like meat,
Did you have no feeling for her?' Where was your empathy?'
But to a member of a grooming gang, no laws had they disturbed,
For the young girls that they preyed on were of so little worth.

And defending lawyers argue then to plead the case away,
'M'Lord my client's culture was what led him astray',
Which just bears out our Shappi's joke about her native land:
'You think Britain has hang-ups – well you should see Iran!'

I write not to stir up anger, but try to analyse,
These awful crimes which perpetrators think are authorised;
And stress the countervalue of the poet's fine ideal:
'Man and woman equal, loving, confident and free'.

Onwards then from Peshawar, and we should have got the train,
Boys threw stones – where learnt they that? – the whole thing was a pain;
But two friendly encounters too, an old man and a guard,
By a bridge made back in Huddersfield in the nineteenth century Raj.

Lahore, one night, and then a bus to the Indian border post
At Wagah, where we there achieved the end we'd wanted most:
To be in the land of India – for that we'd travelled long,
The sight before us proved to us our instincts were not wrong.

India at last

Under the bluest of blue skies, the golden cornfields swayed,
While bunting, touched by gentle winds, in countless colours played;
We had a sense of pleasure that we'd reached our long-sought goal,
With a sense counter-intuitive of somehow coming home.

Amritsar, city of the Sikhs, alive with countless trades,
We sat and watched a passing crowd, a fine wedding parade:
And after pots with fireworks filled had sent up fiery plumes,
Boys would gaily rush at them and kick them without shoes.

Their molten guts then bursting into particles of fire,
Provoking yet more squealed delight, yet lack of adult ire.
No health or safety regulations standing in their way,
A measure of a new milieu where different norms held sway.

That night new money fumbled with, when we paid for our meal,
A gradual relaxation and unwinding we could feel.
Turkey, Iran, Afghanistan, and Pakistan as well,
Had been intense, but now that stress was, thankfully, dispelled.

Next day the Golden Temple standing in its tranquil pool,
Young bucks went by a-smiling and a-joking to us two.
That evening we were fed there in the gurudwara fine,
As volunteers approached us, we were all sat there in line.

And rice and dal and vegetables, and a fine chapati too,
From buckets bright of stainless steel were dished out to the queue.
A custom there for those who passed and of all faiths as well,
Who were like us out on the road and could for three days dwell.

Aside, a giant red hot log under an iron dome,
Chapatis baked and stacked and then whisked off to dining room.
Shining pots of rice and dal were gleaming by the side,
As men and women toiled for us our supper to provide.

And that would introduce us to a side of India,
That would make us feel at home and give us succour there:
A sense that here the wanderer has a respected place,
A kind of status even, and with no sense of disgrace.

Now Kipling has a story in the Second Jungle Book
A Brahmin there – who to the Raj – an oath of fealty took;
He rose to rule but at his height, well, he just disappeared,
Began again out on the road with all his old life cleared

To be a hermit near a village he'd found on his way,
Whose people there had welcomed him and showed him where to stay;
And really, Kipling, you can tell, is trying to explain
The beauty of his choice and of the land from which it came.

Feeling calmed and welcomed, we set off, objective clear,
To reach Dharmsala in the hills now that was our idea.
A bus we took to Pathankot – in the hotel that night,
A woman's laugh, surprising, for months out of sound and sight.

Next afternoon, we climbed on up a half-made rocky trail,
To our left a deep incline where kites and eagles sailed;
In our lungs the fresh air scented by the pine trees green,
White peaks up in the distance and against a blue sky seen.

We stopped to take a rest, looked up and noticed on a branch –
A hunched eagle, magnificent, ignoring our advance;
But finally it launched itself into the setting sun,
Wingbeats supremely effortless, in an instant it was gone.

It was up from Dharmsala that we now were on our way,
To the home of exiles from Tibet, our steps were drawn that day.
McLeod Ganj – its pleasant name and arriving after dark,
We found a lodge and settled in, so glad our things to park!

Next day, the smell of baking bread enticed at our bedside,
We saw around the settlement where all seemed occupied
With chopping wood or weaving cloth where hands in tunics turned
Raw wool to twisted fibre threads to work on roadside looms.

Gleaming cylinders of brass at the centre of the square,
Turned by locals as they passed to send out thoughts and prayers;
Serious pilgrims prostrating themselves stretched out in the dust
Around signs of a culture there refusing to be lost.

So a journal for their nation was in office small produced,
Campaigning for the homeland Chinese communists traduced:
Tales of monks to labour forced and 'when the stars were bright',
Mountain passes told of, with the Dalai Lama's flight.

A ganga-smoking holy man who lived in his own cave,
A Nordic girl with nothing and not quite considered sane;
Good friends in a bungalow who lived further up the hill,
A budding Australian guru – we knew not good or ill.

And there my 20th birthday came, and it sure was a day,
We ate wholemeal bread and honey on a sunlit upland plain.
Two mongeese came and played around much bigger than I'd thought,
A crimson, black and grey wallcreeper by a waterfall.

We went down to the monastery to see a unique sight:
The maroon-clad monks whose chanting made up their daily rites,
Sound that rose and fell and changed and never quite resolved,
Mixed with trumpets, cymbals, bells while prayer wheels revolved.

Then we spent the evening with our good friends up the hill,
Playing guitar at sunset: Nev has got a photo still;
And up the trunk of a pine tree that framed the orange light,
We saw a flying squirrel climb and then launch into flight.

A week or more we stayed on there to revel in the peace,
The mountain air, the friendships, the nice room we'd been bequeathed
By an Australian couple who – the guru was next door –
Had considered Charlie Manson and then thought for them no more.

The plan we formulated was to head for Kathmandu,
See the mountains in their glory and in the season too;
Before that go to Delhi, then Varanasi on the way,
But before we left the mountains, to prolong our foothills stay.

So we headed for Manali, a boneshaking bus ride,
Along the twisting mountain roads that surety defied.
Moralistic traffic signs were obviously ignored –
The wrecks of buses like our own in gorges deep we saw.

Manali, Kullu valley, with the winter coming on,
Mighty trees and moss-strewn floors where shafts of sunlight shone;
An Aussie had a rented house, a fine forest refuge,
And there, Oz helped us out again, for there was room for two.

And so days passed, maybe a week, of walks by forest streams,
Chapatti-making by the fire, fresh air and peaceful dreams,
Talking with our mellow host and exchanging our world-views,
But as the snowline moved on down, we knew we had to move.

But moved too soon … a freezing wait for hours for the coach,
We'd got up much too early and our zeal we sure reproached.
Only when the engine started and slow began to warm,
At last was welcome heat achieved that helped our bodies thaw.

Down in the town of Mandi, we set off in early light,
Passing Shimla in the dark, we reached the plains at night;
Sleeping in a roadside dhaba, on wood and string charpoys,
And waking slowly to the sound of rural India's noise.

A cold and foggy atmosphere, infused with woodsmoke grey,
To catch the morning traffic, we were soon upon our way;
A misty pond with kingfisher, our starting point that morn,
Which our planet home's fine balance then seemed to underscore.

Heading south by evening, to our right the setting sun,
To our left the full moon rising, with imperfections none.
The solar system's movement so perfectly on show,
As the sun dipped out of sight and that full moon arose.

Our Delhi expedition was to change some money there,
A large Sikh money changer at his desk on handsome chair.
Having stayed a night or two and embroidered shirts purchased,
Once more our packs we loaded up with target new to trace.

Hitching the
Grand Trunk Road

Now we had hitched the Grand Trunk Road from Kabul through Lahore
At its westernmost beginnings – now we joined with it once more.
Its flow of life, of goods, of noise – all ruled by lorries loud,
Belching fumes in the hot air and scattering the crowds.

Let me speak of travel with those lorries overflowing:
A wave, not thumb, to indicate we wanted to get going.
'Perceived determination' seemed to be a winning ploy,
And when one lumbered to a halt it always brought great joy.

A driver and his helper then with gleaming friendly smiles,
Images of gurus, gods and woodwork painted bright;
From the windows, birds eye-catching perched on telephone lines,
People walking purposefully with some encumbrance piled.

An hour before sunset, we would slow, come to a halt.
Beside a pond or river there, all clambered out to wash.
Even as the sun went down the washed clothes dried so quick,
Then again back in the cab with the smoke of incense sticks.

To take advantage of cool nights and fairly empty roads,
New drivers joined the convoys and then through the night they drove.
Above the cab with ropes and tyres we could sometimes sleep,
We drifted off under the stars with gently whooshing trees.

Stopping when the morning came and lounging on charpoys,
Bustling, bringing water, snacks – out came all the dhaba boys.
The cook looked so important as the breakfast he prepared,
His wood-fed oven fired up – no effort would be spared.

Onions, garlic, chillies, ginger, fresh coriander chopped,
Spices roasted, toasted, ground and then added in on top.
Then a hefty ladleful of dal from a massive pan,
Sizzled in and odours rich throughout the dhaba swam.

Another oven, dough slapped in to bake chapattis, naan,
A little snooze perhaps after that breakfast had gone down.
Lolling on those charpoys shaded from the morning sun,
Eventually the call 'Chalo' – 'let's go' that is – would come.

So travelling east on lorry top along the Grand Trunk Road,
People looking up and pointing, smiling as we onwards rolled;
One time some sweets and flowers thrown up, an unexpected gift,
A donation of enchantment which gave us such a lift.

But not all was enchantment, for beside the dusty way,
Women, grimy sari-clad, sat breaking rocks all day;
Women, with their children too, and hammering in the dust,
The drivers said their daily wage was five rupees – and just.

India's infrastructure being grown by countless hands,
In the long, long scheme of things all building up the land;
Labourers, miners, engineers – and those road-builders too,
A tipping point would come, I thought, when benefits accrued.

For India had people on its side and when some shining day,
Those energies were harnessed true, then what would people say?
'Can you imagine great-grandmother by the thoroughfare?
She kept our family alive by what she did back there'.

Always sensed, potential in that post-independence land,
A sense of forces gathering, and new routes being planned.
Though marred by the iniquities of caste system unjust,
People just got on with it and earned their daily crust.

Varanasi vistas

One dark night in December, we to Varanasi came,
On the Ganges found a houseboat tethered on the waterway.
In the morning from the roof top by the granite-built north bank,
We looked over the river to unoccupied mud flats.

A giant iron railway bridge the river's width did span,
Soon the river traffic built, each boat a task at hand;
Beside us pied kingfishers hovered, fixed on fish to spear,
While black freshwater porpoises arose and disappeared.

A crow on dead dog's body floated interestingly,
A man with bike was rowed past idiosyncratically;
A goat ate someone's washing, or tried to do, we saw,
A spindly individual twenty punters rowed or more.

Walking then up the potholed bank to walk the narrow streets,
Avoiding water buffaloes that ran the walkways steep;
Then tantalising sights and sounds assailed us thick and fast —
From windows, shopfronts, courtyards, workshops, street scenes that we passed.

Hardware shops with pots and pans there gleamed from front to back,
Drapers' shops with coloured silks resplendently there stacked;
Businessmen in dazzling white under Gandhi's sketch conferred,
Cows ate placidly from stalls till the shopkeeper had words.

Little boys and girls ran for the steaming dung that fell,
Formed it into patties, and then pressed them to the wall;
There to stay in hot sun dried and kept for cooking fire,
While processions bearing shrouded dead moved down towards funeral pyres.

Cremated by the Ganges, to the elements returned;
While living life, so vivid, around those tableaux burned:
Saddhus worshipped Shiva, face paint, loincloths, dreadlocks wild,
By river, clothes were slapped on rocks and on the sandbanks dried.

There were days of sickness and so miserable they seemed,
The street food was delicious, true, but maybe not too clean;
Puri potatoes served in leaves had been a curried treat,
But Delhi belly, as it's known, had knocked us off our feet.

Highs and lows
in the Himalayas

And yet, one day, we packed our things and on time set off to
Fulfil our long-planned aim to reach the fabled Kathmandu.
We may have gone to Patna and even on the train,
But the last part of the journey was sure by road again.

For as Nepal drew near that day, just there before our eyes,
Were the approaching wooded spurs that heralded the rise
Of the mighty Himalaya – and those very spurs and plains,
Showed the crash of continents that took place one long past day.

And then, a night-time lorry ride picked up at border post,
The hours dragged as in the back we shivered in our coats.
Before dark fell, we met a child with belly swollen sore,
We gave him a banana and wished we could do more.

Then in the lorry's open back we jolted through the dark,
The freezing cold, a drawn-out pain, at last we disembarked!
In a fog-bound city square with pagoda roofs around,
Morning risers on the cobblestones, all shitting on the ground.

For two nights we rested up, our energies all consumed,
Venturing out from windowless and tiny hotel room;
Then in Swyambhu down the road, a spacious rural scene:
With a verandah and a view, a friendly family.

With Kathmandu revisited to shoot the city breeze,
We bought something from a street kid with a note of ten rupees.
He said he had no change and that his friend some cash would bring,
That friend then vanished on his bike and left us there waiting.

I'm sure we didn't bully him or act there heavily;
We just thought the transaction would be finished normally;
We asked him when our change would come – he just burst into tears,
And suddenly an angry crowd was battering our ears!

Those shouts turned into punches, kicks – away from them we ran,
An armed policeman turned up then and took us both in hand…
Concluded that as we had run then we had been to blame,
Told us to give him one more note, and sent us off ashamed.

Looking back much later we did not feel we had done wrong,
A situation had flared up with its own updraft strong.
A misunderstanding maybe, perhaps a well-worked ploy,
Between local bystanders and that poor street trader boy.

But anyway, it sure depressed the stuffing out of me,
Cast as the oppressor of the poor in my own mind at least.
After an ascetic Christmas in calming Swyambhu,
We then thought we would separate to give each other room.

We'd been together – now non-stop – for quite three months or more;
We both had a strong feeling that a break could things restore.
We were in a downwards spiral and outside things were strange,
Just that things were all 'tae fock' as my Scots forbears would say.

The temple on the hilltop with concentric rings of gold
Were stages to enlightenment but also, we were told,
Had forced bad spirits off the hill precisely where we were,
That we did not entertain, yet felt unease a-stir.

Off alone to breakfast once an upset man I found,
Lying there face downwards and pawing madly at the ground.
When I asked if I could help at all, some curses were relayed:
All I could do was leave him, and just get on with my day.

A letter at the poste restante from our beloved friends,
Had nothing but bad tidings, although others made amends.
There was nothing from Ann's parents, no, not a single word,
An insufficiency of love, an empty sense for her.

So off I went to Pokhara, then neighbouring Baiwan,
With mighty fishtail mountain peak there towering up behind;
All against a blue, blue sky that showed off its awesome shape,
In front a fine small temple on an island in a lake.

And there I spent New Year with a local family,
Upstairs in their thatched cottage was a lodger's room for me.
Well, up a wooden ladder and then on some flat bamboo,
Below the family there lived with all their livestock too.

They had a raised-up maize stack where the crows would peck all day,
Though obviously their food store they were never chased away.
Little boys would climb the ladder so curious to see,
This visitor from foreign climes and cigarettes to plead.

And there I wrote a New Year song in which I wanted to,
Banish trouble from the world: ridiculous, I knew,
But a kind of cosmic pledge which I would try to meet,
It set me facing forward – new energy, new beat.

I remember two more things, with one of them quite sublime,
When walking out in dawning light a quiet spot to find;
I turned to see the fishtail and its pure eternal snows,
Changed by the sun's first dawning rays to vibrant shining rose.

The next when at the small hotel where evening meals were found,
I heard a bold young native of the USA expound:
How everyone could dollars earn with ease as they did roam,
He'd printed hash shop posters which would sure sell well back home.

Then Ann got back from Kathmandu and our life again resumed,
With peaceful days in Baiwan, I had found a bigger room;
With Ramji and Birendra playing, noticeable too,
Was poor Birendra squatting leaving liquid yellow poo.

So days passed with that family beside that peaceful lake,
White peaks, blue sky and clear-aired rest would wanderlust awake;
We left some things at the hotel to lighten up our loads,
And then set out one morning on the Annapurna road.

I say road, but really, it was more like a little trail,
At valley's foot, large boulders, to the side the waters played;
Ahead of us the white peaks rose up proud against the sky,
They gradually enveloped us as on and up we climbed.

And then the path developed with large paving slabs of stone,
After days of walking, wayside lodges were our home.
Each village isolated, and supplied by porters' packs,
Some mules we saw but mainly it was just those porters' backs.

Sometimes, sadly, oh-so-young, and not a chance of school,
I thought of our insouciance and reckoned we'd been fools
Not to recognise our privilege and use it to the end,
But that's always the way of things, on that you can depend.

Anyway, we moved on up with lodges on the way,
When landslips cut the path we walked, it meant a long delay;
First down over broken earth on the new path we found,
And then again up carefully across the churned-up ground.

And then there were the bridges that could never be ignored,
Three ropes tied together, while beneath the river roared!
Always glad to get across – sometimes porters out of sight
Would tease by gently rocking it to make us both hold tight.

The terraces cut into hills provided growing ground
For the crops of villagers, and at every stop we found
The quality of food was linked to fruitfulness at hand,
So bigger beans and better rice meant more productive land.

A book I read by Tim Marshall, a most impressive chap,
A foreign correspondent for whom nowhere's off the map;
Called 'Prisoners of Geography' it talks of Nepal's fate,
To be landlocked, trapped forever, between its neighbours great.

Communications in the hills are quite a factor too,
Time-consuming, vigour-sapping just getting things to move;
With fertile land a problem too in terms of its sad dearth,
Nepal has natural challenges not easy to disperse.

Its mountains are its assets – they roused wonder and sheer awe,
And getting nearer every day they made us feel so small.
We'd set our sights on seeing the whole Annapurna range,
With Poon Hill and its panorama our specific aim.

One problem – from the outset, we'd been without trekking pass,
We had not done our homework but had set out nonetheless,
And this would have its consequences as you soon will see;
A little psychodrama that would just descend on me.

For as we round a corner came, after a long hard day,
We saw our destination but there standing in the way
Were two policemen on a bridge to see our cards were right,
We knew that we'd be sent on back, and ducked down out of sight.

And there, in wooded enclave and beside the river strong,
Ann found herself a staff and to the rocky bank moved on.
As she, with that puny stick, waded in to test the tide,
I knew I could not follow, sat on a rock and cried.

I knew it was impossible and in that thinned-out air,
With so much at stake it seemed had yielded to despair:
Not only could I never reach our goal and never would,
Ann would go on to great heights, and I'd be left for good.

Such was the stark scenario that played out in my mind.
It dissipated like a dream when I looked up to find
Ann wearily returning and defeated by the tide
Of that rampant, raging, river – one hundred metres wide.

That may have been a moment when she deep inside could see,
In the larger life perspective, we had different destinies.
In confronting giant monsters no effort would she spare,
I'd found her way too reckless, and its danger could not share.

And so, deflated we returned to some stern music face,
But found the guards had packed up, our forebodings were replaced
By knowledge that now Poon Hill was just one day up the path,
So we re-joined our trail buddies and with such lightened hearts.

Jim and George and Ian had become our companions fine –
An Aussie, two Americans – who liked a real good time;
Next day to Ghorepani came, a pass with snowfall deep,
Beneath Poon Hill itself, its height above nine thousand feet.

That evening, the door opened and then with a puff of snow,
In walked a Japanese young man from where I do not know.
He just sat down to meditate and rubbed in forehead balm,
A magical appearance, one which could not help but charm.

Rice and dal and vegetables had become the standard meal,
All served in meagre portions a poor calorific deal.
It's like that in the mountains – for us, just a passing phase,
But for the mountain villagers, a fact for all their days.

Next morning real excited we set off to climb Poon Hill,
An hours' walk up snowbound track and with the air so still.
Up ahead, Ann made her way turning back and cracking jokes;
'Jeez' panted the bulky George, 'she's a full-on mountain goat!'

Approaching to the rounded top a partial sight to see,
Then when we stood triumphant the whole thing was revealed:
Annapurna on the right with its pointed peak of white,
Dhaulagiri on the left a twin wall of tranquil might.

Smaller peaks on either side to the distance did recede,
In front of us a valley vast that plunged so wide and deep:
Green and black and brown it was until its line of snow,
From which in natural majesty the distant peaks arose.

We could not but luxuriate in a sense of triumph real,
All that hard work, toil and angst had been with victory sealed!
The mountains shimmered in clear air into the afternoon,
We sat and chatted happily in front of that rare view.

'Scuse me for being down to earth … but busting for a pee,
(As my Dad would euphemise 'to stand behind a tree');
I found myself so miniscule before those mountains grand,
The cosmos dissolved in one huge laugh as I there did stand

Laughing at the self-concerns that had so pressed in on me,
Truly insignificant and existing laughably;
In bardic words: 'Like a flock of rooks, at a farmer's gun',
They all fled from my poor brain and left me everyone.

I hesitate to claim this an enlightenment at all,
It is a modest insight that we're all just very small.
Our troubles and our worries to be in perspective seen,
And yet, it's helpful to recall the universal scheme.

As afternoon drew on we sensed a change of atmosphere,
Cloud forced up the pass below spilling into the air clear:
In front, behind, encircling us with dire rapidity,
Then a veil across the mountains, one more glimpse – they disappeared!

And suddenly, forthwith we were enveloped in the cloud,
A cold damp world closed in on us, all warmth was disallowed.
The crows croaked in black woods around, the mist swirled too as we
Made our way back downwards taking steps so carefully.

At last, the wooden lodge appeared and by the fire we stayed,
Drained of energy but serene, and thinking of the day:
A matchless spot, unparalleled, with great companions too
And ranked by Lonely Planet in the top ten of world views!

When morning came we set off through the summit of the pass,
Through which the cloud had spilled, to find a wooded downhill path;
Slipping, sliding, taking care – to cope with ice and snow,
The upward climb not easy, but the downwards took a toll.

Finally, with the village reached down on the valley floor
(We'd viewed its roofs from up on high that brilliant day before);
We found the lodge, exhausted, and I took myself to bed,
There with John Lennon's song 'Yer Blues' a-flowing through my head.

The next day we would separate with Ian, Jim and George,
Turning right to Jomoson, still higher up the gorge;
Us turning left to go back down, return from whence we came,
A five or six day journey with the miles melting away.

Sometimes we'd find we'd reached a spot which somehow held us there,
Terraced fields, a hill behind, a sense of concentrated air;
Brightly coloured minivets that flashed in and out of sight,
From the snowline we'd descended now, fit bodies a delight!

Stopped once by a guard, let through though proper pass we lacked,
Under blue skies we descended, the peaks now at our back,
Until one day a bend we turned – there could be no mistake,
Down in the hazy distance was our friendly Baiwan lake.

The last few miles were polished off with such consummate ease,
With our fitness at peak levels the downhill track a breeze;
Relaxing back in Baiwan village for a night or two,
Then a bus back down to India our journey to renew.

So down those wooded spurs we went and reached at last the plain,
By nightfall at the border post, in India again:
A bustling scarcely-lit bazaar – the middle of nowhere,
While Ann and customs man talked deep, to food stalls I repaired.

Austere and awe-inspiring and magnificent, yet strange,
Nepal had just transported me beyond my usual range;
By thinned-out air's effect as well, that took me by surprise,
Upset by hardship, poverty – part of too many lives.

Perhaps a better, humbler person would not have been so phased,
Would not have felt those mountains somehow put him in his place;
And yet the one time I saw Michael Palin quite so stretched and strained,
Was when he was high up filming on the Himalayan range.

And so, a word of warning – visit and enjoy Nepal,
Incomparable and magical, your stay will endure;
Just be prepared for things that come and take you by surprise,
Though they may change you for the better and open up your eyes.

India regained

Next morning, we woke on the platform hard at Gorakhpur,
Waking up with others, hot sweet tea at the station stall;
Remembering, the night before, the hugeness of the dark,
And waiting for a train to pass, its light a distant spark.

Around the bullfrogs croaking in the mighty silence there,
Then its headlight getting closer and scything through the air.
Fifty miles in from the border, yes, a train we had achieved,
Bedded down on platform then and slept – far too tired to dream.

And then the fog of morning – it was winter in the plains –
Was burnt off by the morning sun, and we set off again:
The train to Varanasi, in the same houseboat to stay,
We got our map out on the roof and planned our next assay.

In the Ganges, Ann then washed her hair – an endeavour brave,
For a dead cat floated by next thing, all bloated on the wave!
In truth we were both feeling just a little dull and flat,
Though there were some incidents of note i.e. that floating cat.

Our plans debated, we thought we'd head for Orissa's coast,
To Puri on its shoreline and of which our guide did boast,
Which incidentally, by the way, was disintegrating fast,
Though great, a cheap production which had not been made to last.

So on the road again, but now some travelling tricks we'd learned,
Rice flakes kept to add to tea would help when hunger burned.
Travelling by night was great with the distance eased by sleep,
But daylight hours by engine hot – no break from swollen feet.

The first day, dropped at sundown by a concrete factory,
The land covered by silver dust then taken off to see
George, the Anglo-Indian, he'd sort us out, they thought,
So us to him the villagers they naturally brought.

His face I still remember, and the main room with its bed
Positioned in the middle and with its protective net;
He and his wife insisted that we should sleep there that night,
Quite a thing to give like that but for them that was right.

Thanking them, we left next day and promptly were marooned
By side of road, a long, long time, by waiting blues consumed;
Rescued finally that day when a nifty jeep did slow:
Young magistrates in session took us to their bungalow.

They were there to settle disputes in the locality,
They also settled us in well – a great room for us to sleep;
With iced drinks plied on the verandah in the evening air,
When dark fell a white-clad line brought out the evening fare.

The talk was of rogue elephants, Nixon's impending fall,
The faults of US policy all skewed by the Cold War;
We were truly entertained, well-treated and well-fed,
A chance meeting near Ranchi, weaving shared cultural threads.

Next day a lorry convoy which was for Calcutta bound,
They told us it would travel nearly each mile of the ground
Of the way to Puri, and so we could now unwind,
Enjoy the road with all its life, all thanks to drivers kind.

One day about to start a snake began to cross the road,
The driver turned the engine off and stopped for it to go.
A sacred thing for him perhaps, his duty to defend,
In the roadside brush it disappeared, and he started up again.

Nowhere the chronic malnutrition we'd seen in Nepal,
Though living on the edge, deprived, none seemed to be that poor;
Yet everything was used, recycled – folk skills we agreed –
Showed how in their daily lives no waste could they concede.

The water used for boiling rice went into cattle trough,
To nourish water buffalo with vitamins enough;
And plastic bags created with lit candles fusing seams,
From old tin cans the paraffin lamps or polished rice scoops gleamed.

This I've not forgotten when we'd got back home to the West,
When the tiniest thing is scarce, we all get so upset.
I think back to those Indians making the best of things:
Ingenious, adaptive, using what their shrewdness brings.

Meditative worlds

A night we spent in Cuttack with a hotel room a must,
Cleaned up after our journey and there 'showered off the dust'.
Next found our way to Puri where – right on the Bengal Bay,
A lodging house we stumbled on, a real fine place to stay.

With lots of western travellers who'd come to meditate
At the Kriya yoga ashram near where peace was on the slate;
Peace of mind by ridding it of sentiments impure,
An 'egg-shaped aura' could be made which on them shut the door.

It was most truly definitely a fine sight to see,
Sitting cross-legged travellers who aimed to proper breathe;
Still and concentrating on a goal not to be sought,
With conscious mind but only through unselfconsciousness bought.

A tricky thing for me, in truth, Ann made a better fist,
I've worked it out, my logic, which I think boils down to this:
I find peace in working through the problems that I find,
Achieving that by using not abandoning the mind.

Maybe we were in the doldrums, Ann tried to analyse
In spirit clear the problem, but I did not realise
Actually her purpose was of desiring to restore,
I took it wrong and got upset and set off feeling sore.

And in the city centre by the temple so immense,
Things got more bad-tempered when a bristling Indian gent
Accused me out of nowhere – I, a 'CIA spy now',
I answered back, he took it ill, we had a stand up row.

There'd been it seemed some xenophobic nonsense in the news:
US had nobbled ashrams and was trying them to use.
It had the wrong side taken in the war for Bangladesh,
Had warships sent – India displeased – oh dear what a mess!

One thing I could not stomach from the temple to the sea,
A mile-long wall with cripples lined, beggars and amputees;
Reliant on the temple and on its six hundred cooks,
'It is justice, not just charity' to which the virtuous look.

We were now in February and in a February state of mind,
It was not just us, one day 'back home' a couple I did spy;
On the way back from the city, 'You *pig*,' her sore complaint,
He looking down and sheepish – truly put into his place.

But there was much to be enjoyed, we never got to that,
Beach awakenings, wrested by hot sun from sleeping bags;
Full lotus stiff-backed meditators, facing the sunrise,
Banana pancakes at the gate, a little enterprise.

Good company back at the lodge with Hindu thinking praised,
'Do not underestimate' was the message there relayed.
Folk far more settled in than us (with traveling bug imbued):
'We always wait for the full moon and then the next one too'.

Once, for evening ritual, to a local shrine called round,
In darkness sat with smoke and fire and gongs that did resound;
The ceremony over, sadhus yogic muscles flexed,
Lifting themselves off the ground legs crossed behind their necks!

But one thing that we missed out on, a real great pity too,
The Sun Temple at Konarak which beneath our radar flew,
And Bodh Gaya, where Buddha gained enlightenment, we'd missed,
I don't know quite what happened, our antennae so remiss.

But these things happen sometimes – on the Isle of Wight I heard,
Someone at the festival – this was his solemn word:
He'd sadly dropped off waiting for Jimi Hendrix to play,
When he awoke all over – and he was dead in seven days!

South by hook or crook

Anyway, the time moved on, and the time came to depart,
We got out on the road and made a creditable start.
'Well we've hitch-hiked all round Scotland and this is just the same –
We'll hitch hike all round India without the slightest pain!'

But at Vishakapatnam, the comparison broke down,
The distance was just so immense, and a station there we found…
Bought our tickets to Madras but still not properly booked,
It turned out that the proper reservations we had overlooked.

'Allowed because foreigners' the inspector did then sign,
Our ineptly bought tickets and so seats we got – how kind!
It was our first train journey long on 'Indian terrain',
(A well-known clothing brand name too, I find I have to say).

Anyway, joking aside, in the carriage now we found
We occupied the centre stage, the questions flew around:
'Are you married?' 'Have you children?' 'How long in India been?'
'Do you know my uncle's friend who lives in Aberdeen?'

No need now for the rice flakes which had been our last refuge,
Appearing, re-appearing food with an assortment huge:
Tea, samosas, coffee, biscuits, pakoras, full meals too,
Orders taken, then passed on, veg or non-veg you could choose.

That Coromandel Express train took fourteen hours long,
Though when dawn came and tea came round, we then looked out upon
The slowly-passing dwellings of Madras and its outskirts,
And soon in the central station all passengers dispersed.

In a churchyard by the long beach, we could put up our tent,
For a family connection had smoothed things out ahead.
Our wee blue tent, the whitewashed church, behind the blue, blue sea,
Each morning, crowds of local kids their breakfast to receive.

'Meter coffee' in the caffs a spectacular folk skill,
Ganesh, Shiva, Jesus, gurus behind the wall did fill.
Some wags apparently will say John F. Kennedy too
In their displays of deities, they can't help but include.

There was a quieter, calmer feel to everything around,
More polite and ordered, more spoken English to be found.
R.K. Narayan redolent, with small-town quality,
Those of different faiths and none, co-existing peaceably.

Of course we'd loved the kids who kicked the fireworks, slapped down dung,
The energy, vitality, so picturesque and fun!
Yet here the neat school crocodiles, the plaits and uniforms,
Laid foundations of contentment with breaks and chances born.

Ok, man, I'm going straight but nobody should exist
To be fodder for the flâneur – now that we should resist.
Indeed the fruits of what we saw can here be seen today,
Doctors in what's Chennai now treating folk in USA.

'Straightlaced, staid' the Mumbaikars groan, when relocated there,
The contrast with their humming home can drive them to despair.
Yet we enjoyed its discreet charm and non-oppressive feel;
We could live without being seen as some enormous deal.

And actually, there were some times out of the ordinary.
On the bus and out of town a sudden piercing scream;
Someone had robbed a woman's purse immediately we found,
The driver took swift action and turned the bus around….

Drove straight to the police compound, behind the gate clanged fast,
Police entered to search all those who near to her had passed.
Alas! They could nothing find, we proceeded on our way,
She'd lost a lot of money too, for her, a real bad day.

And at the Theosophical Society we found,
A venerable banyan tree roots dropping to the ground;
And golden backed woodpeckers there, a-tapping at the trees,
Mongeese, hoopoes, cormorants, all with a cooling breeze.

Oh my gosh, I do remember one time I took a dip
In the sea on the long beach and found the currents ripped
Me quite from my footings to be in swirling water found,
But then a huge wave picked me up and I felt solid ground.

We had a tiny compact stove, and breakfast, lunch we made,
But went at night to café near where good food was arrayed.
And at Mahabalipuram, the memory's still bright,
We tasted coconut chutney, that went with dosa right!

The road out to that beach retreat, now that's still in my mind,
A single track of tarmac there protruding from the sand;
The sea to left, a pale blue sky and casuarina trees,
The hot, hot sun but finally a gentle cooling breeze.

This time we were more clued up, to shore temple repaired,
And sculptures fine in solid rock we *did* home in on there.
The temple moderately small but made so beautifully,
Standing its form perfect, black stone weathered by the sea.

We slept out on the dunes at night, and sheltered in the days,
Chanced on other travellers, one a US alpha-male.
One evening by the temple stones, beneath the stars I played,
My Mahabalipuram gig still legend there today!

There were some final sunsets from the ridge that looked inland,
Over water, palms and paddy fields – then we had to plan
For our returning journey as our farthest point we'd reached,
Now we were heading north and west, no longer south and east.

A Goan interlude

So, in Mahabalipuram – at last we packed to go,
Knowing every travelled mile would take us nearer home;
And from Madras to Bangalore and then on west again,
To reach Panjim in four hard days – now ninety mins by plane.

But travelling in India repeatedly contrasts
The heat and dust with havens pure that in the memory last;
And so we found, with Goa's shores so gruellingly reached,
Our blue tent now was proudly pitched by the Anjuna beach.

On a terrace, on an outcrop, under a grove of palms,
We looked out on a stretch of sand where waves lapped soft and calm.
A local came, shinned up the palms, to us their fruit he brought,
At night the sound of gentle waves that washed away dark thoughts.

And in this placid paradise a whole week we could spend,
Though soon becoming cognisant too much of it could lend
A despondent air to residents who with no trouble stayed –
Ann thought there was too little to keep the mind engaged.

No dharma class as in McLeod, no Puri ashram room,
A Frenchman snared by opium, enshrouded in his gloom;
A young American, who in McLeod was a live wire,
Now seeming drained by India, grey-faced and uninspired.

But two Australian girls stopped over, open-hearted, brave,
(Our tent attracting visitors who did our spirits save!)
They inspired a little poem and got us back on track:
Against the unexpected mood, we determined to fight back.

So we explored the rockpools with their creatures so bizarre,
Cooked suppers on an open fire underneath the stars;
Wrote messages upon the beach: 'All things must pass' was mine,
Ann thought it much too gloomy – I reckoned it was fine.

And the beach bars were spectacular in their laid-back way,
Chai and coffee, masala fish fry, tables in the shade;
A dreadlocked sadhu admirable, athletic and well-formed,
With his Swedish girlfriend, human beauty in their bond.

Eventually we set off north, the hill behind to climb,
Wondered at a ruined fort and a ferry caught in time!
Crossed the Chapori river then up the beach for miles,
Rocks extending needle-like, a signal we'd arrived.

For there behind – a hidden lake just inland from the sea,
Fresh water, shallow, sheltered by surrounding hills and trees;
The fiery sun creating tiny rainbows on its floor,
There moving with the ripples when the wind its surface scored.

Kingfishers, pied, electric blue, dived in for tiny fish,
Which were nourished by the food scraps from every washed up dish.
There were, I guessed, near twenty of us living round the lake,
Impressed on all no soap to use to save its limpid state.

Cashew trees a wonder, with their fruit apple-like green,
The one reminder of the world some tankers out at sea;
Sun getting up, so none could walk with bare feet on the sand,
At night a perfect image from Mr Tambourine Man.

On up, past the cashew trees, where the jungle trees began,
A path led to a special place – a solitary banyan:
A sacred place for villagers, a place of peace we found,
Where we could close our eyes and just take in the world around.

Like being underwater, tree tops surface of the sea,
Spring growth, Nature reasserting all its vitality.
Soft rustlings around us, sunlit patterns on the ground,
Chipmunks chasing, green shoots sprouting, bird song all around.

Then the equilibrium broken by a crashing sound,
In the distance coming nearer, alarming too we found:
A troupe of monkeys making its way down the sloping hill,
Through the tree tops travelling, their noise the senses filled.

Then fading to the distance and the quietness returned,
At last, we'd walk back to the lake, again the sand would burn;
I wrote there, 'Silence at last', with need for true peace slaked,
Those my last recollections of Goa's Arambol lake.

Last days in Agra

With April come, regretful, we set off with sense of loss,
Petrol engines met with once the Chapori river crossed.
Whitewashed churches, beaches, palm trees – all now left well behind,
The sensory assault of India once more we'd find.

One thousand kilometres plus read one disheartening sign,
As through Bombay we passed somehow, the northwards road to find;
Our target new was Agra, to be our last sojourn,
On the way out to the border, swan song before return.

And then we caught a convoy moving at a mighty clip,
We covered it in just two days: a real impressive trip!
The hill forts on the clifftops are my only memory,
And soon we were in Agra with the Taj Mahal to see.

And furthermore, to pick up mail – in the post office grounds,
A worker there, a Christian, to his house asked us around;
And there his family laid on for us an Easter meal,
All standing by and smiling in true hospitality.

Mahabalipuram's shore temple, called 'lyric in stone',
As a 'symphony in marble' Agra's glory could be known.
A monument to love and made in perfect symmetry,
Built to preserve a love, existing just in memory.

Which is a cue for – no, that would be moving on too fast,
The story must stay true to time with all in proper class;
So now, my pleasant duty is to tempt and lure you where,
To the lodgings with a family, we had both repaired.

A wired-off verandah with a real fine outside view,
A garden with life teeming, lizards, chameleons too;
Golden backed woodpeckers there, a-hammering on the trees,
Pink hoopoes with their rounded wings and long curved-downwards beaks.

It was a moment when to weigh up India we tried,
Ann making lists of sight and sounds which memory supplied;
But also to anticipate the journey sure decreed –
The cash in our possession did not twenty pounds exceed.

One image last must be recalled: as I sat in the town,
In a dirt poor desperate slum with rubbish tips around—
Scabby dogs and needy kids and shacks with palm roofs low,
Showed for sure that India still had so far to go.

But now the heat was building with two showers or more a day,
Absolutely vital as it made its steady way
Towards the truly unbearable, and finally we left
In April leaving India and feeling quite bereft.

Jaundiced journeying

And so a hotel in Lahore, and then a ticket booked,
Because of dire finances one we had to overlook;
But into Quetta's stationmaster emphatically we bumped,
He sussed us out, and in his station office we were dumped.

An imposing man with jacket white on which the buttons gleamed,
He clapped his hands and soon his servant came with cups of tea;
And we showed him all we had, and he must have thought I guess,
For Pakistan's train service we had tried to do our best.

For he let us go, we left with a pleasant memory,
(He had even given lemon cream biscuits with the tea!)
And then a minibus we took to cross Baluchistan
On that desperate desert road for the border with Iran.

Now we were five from Pakistan, and from Italy two,
An Irishman with life-enhancing kick-ass attitude.
Things started well in morning cool, but heat intensified,
With that hot sun then strengthening, we felt the tensions rise.

But even if so few and far, there were some rest stops too,
Water dark and brackish, a meagre roti chai menu.
And at one stop, where as one does, one's functions to relieve,
I looked down and noticed a stream of vivid orange pee.

At once I knew this signified a hepatitis state,
I'd had a jab but sadly it was long since out of date.
Maybe those sweets of grated ice, all topped with sweetened cream,
Had not been a good idea – where had that water been?

So now it was official, I had not been feeling hale,
But now the hep had been confirmed I felt my spirits fail;
Anyway, now what to do but keep on keeping on,
Towards that Iranian border post and then on to Zahedan.

Ann saw my eyes were yellow bright, we made a little plan,
To hold it all together till we got back to Tehran.
Not ideal conditions, for no rest till then could there be,
But the other musts – no drink, no fat – we could those achieve.

It was now that our Irish friend continued to insist
On rolling joints, long after he'd been told he must desist.
Told he would be left out there and a magistrate must see,
He scorned the contradictions and yet had to accede.

And it was after sunset that we reached the border post.
The Irish guy, a lecture read, was all that they could boast:
'That's not a proper magistrate,' said he with scornful lip,
But honour then was satisfied and off to eat we slipped.

That border post in nowhere-land on charpoys there to lie,
Something godforsaken or…did I have a jaundiced eye?
Anyway, the day came up with a long wait for the bus,
And right on cue, a sandstorm fierce then blew right up on us.

Now when those girls from Bethnal Green set out to Isis find,
That miserable choking sandstorm came right back to mind:
'Don't do it girls, just keep your schools and keep your families;
Keep your running water, power and well-stocked libraries'.

'That Caliphate is just a dream, and of distempered minds,
An empire like the Ottoman you never more will find;
In history's long unfolding that one for sure is binned,
Like the Confederacy of old – it's just "Gone with the Wind".'

It was only after dark that we got to Zahedan,
We met a friendly soldier there who took us both in hand.
Through alleys dark he led us on, our instincts we did trust,
That night, in deepest Zahedan, he kindly put us up.

Next day, ahead a journey, of near seven hundred miles
To the Iranian capital, and so with our packs we filed
To that dusty desert road, and soon a brand new truck
With gizmos gleaming everywhere, then stopped and picked us up.

The lorries back in India had been of basic build,
Rudimentary maybe – patch ups easy to fulfil.
On this ones' snazzy gearstick though some gizmo went awry,
There's a lesson in there somewhere, but what, I can't decide.

Three days of hard, hard travelling, hep not a bit of fun,
One evening from the lorry falling absolutely done!
Then sick into a flowerbed, exhausted lost and lorn,
A couple young there took us in and hosted us till morn.

So when you see those screaming crowds, all calling for the death
Of America, of England with spittle-lobbing breath;
There's kindnesses and goodness too amongst those people found,
Though often overridden now, they'll surely come back round.

For, to recap, we had been put up three times in Iran,
That shepherd, and then that soldier, and now near to Tehran.
In Afghanistan, near Kandahar and rescued in Paghman,
A respite in Jalalabad with that car-driving wealthy man.

I think that night we'd been put up, we were approaching Qom,
Not too distant from Tehran – we were there next afternoon.
A hotel with a large, shared space, and lots of friendly folk,
There I collapsed and went to bed, felt bad, it was no joke.

And our finances when we looked were absolutely dire —
In fact our pride we swallowed and to embassy retired.
They booked us on a nice fast train to Istanbul again;
Soon a taxi to the station (with us) its way did wend.

With businessmen Iranian was our compartment shared,
One loaded with pistachios – ten kilos full were there!
He shared them out and everybody sure did treat him well,
Until all gone when – dear, oh dear! – they then would give him hell.

One time – in eastern Turkey then – the train stopped at Lake Van,
So we got out to stretch our legs and have a look around.
We were in eastern Anatolia: wow, that was a thing!
Around us birch trees, snow-capped peaks, and every sign of spring.

For now we were in early May – the year had come around,
Eight months since our departure, now we were homeward-bound!
As we revelled in the scenery with the train still there in view,
To our horror it then started up and – oh no! – began to move.

'Should we not run?' our friend enquired, and after it we ran!
To be stranded in Anatolia on the far shore of Lake Van
Did not appeal, but luckily it then slowed to a halt,
And we returned to precious seats and laughed at that rude shock.

Now in Madras Ann had acquired – for only three rupees,
A little knife she rated – an American agreed;
So as we sat in restaurant car, a twenty dollar bill,
Was passed across the table there, our coffers to refill.

It was a four day journey, and in Istanbul once more,
We stayed one night, and then again were by the city walls –
Embarking on the final lap, me feeling just ok,
But that journey back to London, on mind and body weighed.

With Yugoslavia going on, then on and on for miles,
I had to leave the lorry once and puke by the roadside.
And then the road through Austria, with mountains seeming small,
In Germany, two hundred kph on the dashboard!

Next through the lands of northern France, the dead still in the air,
'A good German's a dead German', one driver would declare.
And so Ann saw me back to home – a decent thing to do,
And next day we just parted, we knew that we were through.

I think that there was little said, I'd just felt her recede—
Turn to a different future with her own distinctive needs.
The yoga thing, a key for her I could not really share,
Our joint endeavour ended: there was no incentive there.

Well I had always thought we'd have a kind of proud return,
Having sailed the seven seas, with so much wisdom learned!
Ann and I would be together continuing along,
Unruffled and enlightened, a source of sense and calm.

But those pious expectations had vanished in thin air—
I was ill, we had split up, now there was no one there.
The first break-up always the worst, a world finished, denied,
But I would work my way through it, and find the other side.

Hard landing, recommencing

Now those beloved friends I mentioned, way back in Nepal,
They'd now set up a commune in a village way up north.
We all felt estranged I guess, but just like a family,
There we found a natural answer to our internal needs.

But it was not easy for me, and Ann was still around,
New friendships, new excitements when I was so earth-bound.
I was a disappointment to the communes' leading lights,
They had some kind of vision – for me, something wasn't right.

There had been a subtle shifting I could not understand,
Having been at distance from events in my own land.
An end to growth unlimited, a now impending change,
To the confident assurance in progress unrestrained.

Because – back from Keats's time, there had been an upward swing,
An impetus from industry that would great prospects bring;
Given still more influence by the harnessing of oil—
The aftershocks from Yom Kippur had those assumptions spoiled.

With the tipping point arriving that winter when we'd missed
The three-day week, power cuts, ends to Empire's privilege,
With such assumptions punctured came a new world and untried,
Now needed skills to navigate an unfamiliar tide.

I often think of good John Leach who really helped me there,
Just said 'Well, you're ill, you know,' when I was in despair.
That was a truly helpful thought that helped to see me through,
When he died in Australia I had lost a friend so true.

He sure deserves a tribute verse: his smile with amused eyes,
His unforced generosity, his beatnik ways precise;
His immersion in the Grateful Dead, their cerebral beauty
Reflecting on his inner self, setting his spirit free.

And in the Yarra river, to the elements returned,
Becoming part of Nature, in no sepulchre interned;
Like those at Varanasi, dispersing in the air,
Or a 'ripple in still water' that's still in motion there.

Back then, the inner workings that the blood will clean for you
Were not functioning properly, my mind and brain were skewed.
It seemed to take an age and it might well have been a year,
But finally, the jaundiced fog would simply lift and clear.

Now while away, I'd written songs, arranging them in groups,
And in Norwich I'd encountered a new endearing troupe;
And music there was everywhere, it had a hopeful feel,
I worked nights in a factory and bought a reel to reel.

But still I found it difficult, to tear myself away,
I tried one-time, and then again, but finally one day
Announced that I was leaving – when I told Ann I'd be gone,
I sensed her disappointment – I might be completely wrong…

For though she'd embarked on her own life, I was kind of there,
Still with a tie to her perhaps, now that beyond repair.
Though after I'd to Norwich moved, she came to visit me,
Said she thought me 'really sussed' – in the end she'd also seen,
That Langley Park could not fulfil, though she her friends would miss,
She sat and told us of her plans and left me with a kiss.

Now that there 'Dorothea' song, of course, by Taylor Swift,
About young friends and parting – now's the right time to enlist:
'I got nothing but well wishes for ya', she sings so fine,
Stating views for Ann, and all that remain to this day mine.

In Norwich I met Dave Eastoe, a fine musician he,
The songs got life, and each became a little entity;
Within 30 months of my return, we were up on stage,
Supporting the great John Martyn: a huge thrill at our age.

Then the fascinating Shelley, so much traduced was found,
To make his work available, I then felt duty-bound;
To sneak him into daily life by pop-songs of the day,
That was my plan and towards that goal I slowly made my way.

So now Shelley has an album, John Keats a single too,
And Byron's freedom ride in Greece is there for all to view.
An album 'Finding a Way Through' with words of mine in songs,
Instinctive ways of working towards that glimpse of ended wrongs

That had flashed up that New Year past, at Baiwan in Nepal,
With people, so free, dancing round a blazing bonfire all;
'Were I a Magician' just an apprentice work for sure,
But one that would lay out for me the road that stretched before.

Looking back

In conclusion, well I humbly feel it should recorded be,
That we had hitched our merry way, so ecologically,
First from London to Istanbul, through France, Italy, Greece,
Then back again near eight months on to where our journey ceased.

And the exotic Grand Trunk Road from Kabul to Lahore,
The Khyber Pass along the way, I'll never see it more.
From Mandi through to Kathmandu, with hellish night-time ride,
Varanasi to Orissa's shore washed by the Bengal tides.

Puri to Visakhapatnam, where we quit and took the train,
Then from Madras to Lahore, back in Pakistan again;
On from Zahedan to Tehran, blighted by hep for me,
From Istanbul to London as mentioned previously.

So thanks to all the drivers who had kindly picked us up,
I hope we were good comrades, we were glad with you to sup!
Thank you to the kind souls who gave us shelter on the road,
We were supremely vulnerable, to the world we were exposed.

You could say that we saw the best, and maybe too the worst,
Making judgements speedily, in that we soon were versed.
Our instincts largely right, humanity commonly fine,
A sense of natural justice in which we could trust most times.

But not that night in Paghman when accosted in our tent;
Years on I got an explanation of that incident
When working in a department store with an Iranian,
Whose mother tongue was Farsi, shared with Afghanistan.

I'd remembered them repeating one word insistently,
He confirmed its sexual meaning and looked so strange at me.
And so we'd had a great escape, it still gives me a chill,
But also, satisfaction that we'd thwarted their ill-will.

Our journey somewhat indirectly would then lead me to
A marriage to a daughter of vibrant Tamil Nadu,
Who basically saved my life in more ways than twenty three;
And welcomed me into her life and to her family.

And since we wed, of course, we've then to India returned,
I've watched it change, develop, grow, take many twisting turns;
And that has been a constant thing that works against the gloom,
People taller, better fed, and slum-dwellings cleared too.

Now here a tale I'll tell you: thirty years to the day
After we'd departed Agra and I'd just sadly gazed
On rubbish tips and children poor and shacks with palm roofs low,
I left India once again but this time thinking how

A ride we'd had the night before, home through the Chennai streets,
In a new Mercedes – though not a sign of equity;
Yet demonstrated movement, progress, advance of a sort –
The Triumph and Ambassador were all that could be bought

When we'd made our journey – and when those wistful dreams
Of advancement and potential had seemed capricious gleams,
Now something was a-stirring sure, with headway being made,
Well-dressed young, so confident on Independence Days.

Of course, it's now not all like that and poverty remains,
But the steady growth has carried on, in my perspective plain:
Machinery and industry a bigger force than then,
Schools imparting skills upon which sundry lands depend.

With that the hoopoes by the road are now – well hardly seen,
The golden backed woodpeckers in retreat from urban scenes.
Those hillside stations like McLeod Ganj built-up tourist sites,
Arambol Lake in Goa now which shops and restaurants blight.

And yet, and yet, there's beauty in the lives that can expand,
Through the livings that result – that I do understand;
And places where one can write simply of – 'Silence at last',
Will always be in India – consigned not to the past.

I think the advertising for the Indian Tourist Board,
Will say India will change you, and strike a hidden chord.
Indeed, that's right, I've not forgotten all those varied scenes:
That hidden chord's still sounding on, still ringing out in me.

Real-time writings

<u>Iran</u>

Hitching through the desert on the Asian Highway
The road to Afghanistan
We're together in mind and bodies
Travelling without a plan
And the way that the moon comes out of the evening
Takes you right outside of your mind
The red sun, rising into the morning
And there's nowhere else to find

<u>Afghanistan</u>

This is a song about a very fine place
Called the Peace Hotel Kandahar
Where everyone's sitting around
Laughing and playing guitar, ah ha!
Laughing and playing guitar.

Well the pines are green against the deep blue sky
And the evening's full of peace…

In sunny Kabul
I was
Losing some weight,
I was
Losing some hate,
I was
Finding the centre to my mind,
Plenty of time…

Ann sitting there
Sun in her hair
Me wondering why my songs

Are all about me—
Very unhealthy…

Pakistan

Molten golden streams the sun
Through the wooden doorway
Sacred sunsets light diffusion
Through smoke of gold and grey—

And the birds are flying
Away from the sun…
Rolling away, away from the day.

The sun of a luminous gold
Sliding away down a peak of a mountain

India

Feeling alone and far from home
With a head about to explode,
Looking for peace in the crowded streets…

Then we got to Dharmsala
Everyone's reading the Dharma
Expecting good karma

There's a feeling locked in my body
That I'm trying hard to find—
It's a feeling of inner peace
And serenity of mind

When your earthly troubles melt away
To a deep pool of calm
And spaces between friends are filled
And barriers laughed down.

Sleeping on top of a lorry,
Stars and trees flashing by,
Bamboo leaves gently waving
Against the light blue sky.

Emerald winged kingfishers,
Camels and monkeys too;
A swan in evening colours
Flying into view.

That's India,
Or a little bit of what we found
And if you go yourself
It'll turn your head around!

Nepal

Were I a magician,
I would free all people
And watch them dance, released from their chains;
Were I an enchanter,
I would re-kindle laughter
In the eyes of those burdened with pain.

Were I a musician
I would sing of the beauty
Of the dawn, and again of the eve;
And if I were a dancer
I would dance in the water
And the pure air of ecstasy breathe.

If I were a jester
I would laugh at the emperors
And spit at their courts and their crowns;
And if I were the lightning,
If I were the lightning,
I would strike all their fortresses down!

If I were a healer,
I would heal in the markets—
The old and the lame and the blind;
And if I ever find serenity
I'll be strong and gentle and kind.

<u>India regained</u>

I left a bit of my ego on top of Poon Hill
It happened when I went to have a pee,
For the mountains suddenly heaved and shaked
And started laughing at me.

Well their Himalayan happiness freaked me for a second
I didn't know quite what to do,
And then I realised what they were laughing at
And I burst out laughing too!

So if you're travelling to Nepal's Poon Hill
Take a look into the snow;
For two footprints and a yellow patch
Mark where I learned to go with the flow.

(Goa – Anjuna)

The eyes flicker
Listening
Not afraid
Glistening…

(Goa – Arambol lake)

Such a pure place,
The mornings are so gentle.
Shade and golden water,
A little spring nearby;

Brown bodies and smiles
And thoughts floating by
Silence, at last!

(Agra)

I can't express my love
But it sings for itself
As yours does
So I think you'll understand.

She's not a girl, she's a woman
And she brings with her an area of peace:
Flowers twisted in her hair,
Wood doves gathering around her feet

And when she comes towards you
Smiling welcome,
Her colours and her wisdom and her warmth
Replace fears and memories of failure…

This moment life is living all around me
A lizard frozen on the wall…

Afterwords I:
Poems and songs
1975 – 2021

Norwich: 'You gotta serve somebody'
Nottingham: John Martyn encountered
London: 32 Milford St as was
Italian interlude: Palinuro, Tavarnelle, Catania
Madras '89
Bombay Moon
Seringapatam
Iran: In this place of blue and gold: for Omar Khayyám
Pakistan: Osama Bin Laden: A Byronic epitaph
India: The Ballad of Akbar and Aurangzeb
      La Ballade d'Akbar et d'Aurangzeb
'Beatles Ashram', Rishikesh 2014
Chennai, 2014
Asian Highway
Marriage song
Don't think Black, don't think White

To round off this collection and to create enough pages to make a paperback edition feasible I include two sections of 'Afterwords', comprised of poems or song lyrics written since our journey.

'Afterwords I' includes around 16 poems or song lyrics drawn from the world of 'On the Asian Highway'. 'Afterwords II' includes poems and songs from a later, perhaps darker era, looking for what Keats called the 'particles of light in the midst of a great darkness'.

The first three are drawn from my early life in Norwich and London, and include a poetic assessment of John Martyn as encountered in Nottingham. Some little verses about a visit to Italy in the late 1970s sneak in (after all we did pass through Italy didn't we); 'Madras '89' records my return to India following my marriage, fifteen years after leaving.

The next poems are roughly in chronological order: 'Bombay Moon' is a kind of non-Manichean poetic approach to the issue of colonialism as it has washed over India. One night, in a residential high-rise flat I found myself thinking of the city's famous Gateway to India and used it as a way of introducing a series of different arrivals in the country. Modern pilgrims like The Beatles, 'intent on changing night to day', next the Parsis, driven from Persia in the 7th century after the Muslim conquest, then the women travelling to India from Britain during the Raj for marriage. We had visited both coasts on that trip, and saw north of Madras a Dutch cemetery, with its heart-breaking children's tombs and of young soldiers too. Off the coast of Kerala by the Arabian sea we saw the enticing, perilous rocks out to sea that emphasised the perils of the trading and colonial ventures that India's riches provoked.

Seringapatam is a name that evokes the more ruthless aspect of British involvement in India. Tipu Sultan, who had sided with the French against the East India Company, was besieged in his fortress there and killed when British and allied forces broke into his stronghold. On a visit there (Srirangapatna today) I was suffering from an upset tummy and took to bed with recent religious controversies running though my head.

Iran is represented by a poem for Omar Khayyám, delivered for the Omar Khayyám Club in the splendid surroundings of the ballroom at the Savile Club in London. The mind of the Persian astronomer, poet, and sceptic found a home in that of the Suffolk-based Edward Fitzgerald, whose translation of his Rubaiyat gave him global prominence, even being (mis)quoted by Bill Clinton.

Lord Byron wrote scathing epitaphs for political opponents; a slightly less cutting version for Osama bin Laden, killed of course in Pakistan, is included. It hinges on the disparity between the Islamist rhetoric about paradise ('a flimsy pretence', as Byron put it) and being in love with death - and the actual reactions at being dispatched to that much-vaunted fate.

'The Ballad of Akbar and Aurangzeb' focuses on two Moghul Emperors whose careers seem to encapsulate the two faces of contemporary Islam. Akbar tolerant and intellectually curious, debating with those of other beliefs, Aurangzeb the polar opposite with a well-attested record of intolerance and persecution. Akbar, the lyric suggests, is a model for contemporary Muslims living in a pluralistic environment. It is also included in a French translation (with thanks to everyone who helped).

Visiting the still-standing buildings of the ashram complex in Rishikesh in 2014 it was good to think of The Beatles, who after all worked their socks off during their career, getting some thinking space with the gentle sound of the Ganges in the background. In the same year, back in Chennai, a three year-old boy lost his mother – such a tragedy! – but the poem hopes for the best possible outcome, nevertheless.

I had used that moment approaching the Afghan border to open a song tracing our journey through to northern India; when told by my brother-in-law that I'd got the astronomical details (about Orion) all wrong I took the opportunity to rewrite it and give it a retrospective flavour. 'Marriage song' was written to celebrate the marriage of my wife's nephew in Kerala, and finally 'Don't think Black, don't think White' proposes that actually, humanity is all one in spirit, heart and mind.

Norwich

'You gotta serve somebody'

The spirit of poetry's there flowing through me,
She ever enjoins me to act in her name;
To speak to the people, to act across borders,
To achieve for her children what men know as fame.

In a top upstairs room in a squat up in Norwich,
I remember so clearly the day that she came;
And shook me inside with a sense of her power,
And lifted me up with her bright-burning flame.

And from that day onward, I followed her prompting,
For richer, for poorer, in sickness and health;
There are times when she leaves me, and takes up with others,
And times when she showers me with spiritual wealth.

Nottingham

John Martyn encountered

A man of vital paradox, a rugby player at school,
A face of hippie wistfulness with another visage duelled;
Growling, moaning, vocalising from some hurt inside,
Honest beyond honesty with nothing feared to hide.

Waves of sound sent crashing out, just one man with guitar,
Rocking backwards in his chair, entranced in world afar;
Fingers flying, slapping, climbing, notes many or few,
Cascading layers of pulsing sound sent washing over you.

And then he laughs, and makes a joke and throws it all away,
Shows he's human after all, the tension then assuaged;
Held the hall right in his hands his power to unify,
And then a song that gently touches everyone inside.

'Oh John had demons' said his friend who'd played with him in clubs,
His manager advancing wads of cash for damages to pubs;
His wife a troubled history to speak of in their lives,
Friends' faraway expressions when this they tried to clarify.

Part Glaswegian hard man, part Home Counties soft,
Childhood letters to his Mum with heart-breaking sense of loss;
And yet the cards dealt out to him he played as best he could,
A tolerant compassion kindness twisting through his roots.

And here he was in Nottingham - and being the main man,
His presence helping raise some funds for some youthful fans;
Absolutely there for them in all complexity,
And here straightforward giving out with no tricks up his sleeve.

Finishing with 'Solid Air' he held the room transfixed,
Pride in his unique quality 'no one taught me this'!
After all a song for his friend for whom he deeply cared,
And backstage in the dressing room he spoke with music there.

London

32 Milford Street as was

Where I came to live and work,
Was a piece of sinking London town;
The cars on the surrounding roads,
Like currents leaving us aground.

The apples formed upon the trees,
Hiding derries, only seen
When winter stripped away the green—
And empty windows grinned and gurned
Gothic in their sad decay,
While every moment, every day,
Aviation's grind and boom
Stole quiet from my tiny room.

The dogs fought, the children screamed,
The simple tunes announced ice cream;
Life went on with youth so free,
Immune to looming destinies.

And here the grass and sycamores
Thrust into the tarmacc'd land;
While a helmet, vintage World War Two
Old and holed and rusted through,
Told of past and harder times—
The war, the blitz, and Nazi crimes.

There went Gladys, like a ghost,
Once a civil servant she;
Sleeping rough, but haven found,
In our blithe society.

Now the street reverberates -
It is the kids come back from school;
With noise and shouts they let off steam

And sometimes bricks and bottles flew
Towards Leopold's house, a few doors down.

Somewhat crazed and absent he,
In a darkened house with friendships few;
Far from Niger, far from home,
Life had led him to a life alone.

He once came out with iron bar,
And hurled it towards his foes so young;
Now he emerges, screams abuse,
Dispersing those who wished him wrong.

This is not winter, autumn's here,
Our thoughts tinged with uncertainty:

Memories of cold and whistling winds,
That banged the corrugated fence;
And how the onset of the dark,
Could turn our world to violence.

Three gentle junkies, beaten up
Over a drug deal all gone wrong;
The neighbours' punch ups in the street,
Their crazy alcoholic song;

So the cops would come, they just had time
(Burdened as they were with crime)
To stop, then roll their windows down,
And chide the fighters on the ground.

But soon prevarications came:

'Ok lads, we must be gone -
There's a robbery up at Clapham South';
So that one just got left to Ron
(Who had the bulk) to sort it out.

With the waning of the light

The derries seemed to say:
'We were built, and had our day,
When power was in England's hand,
But growth is followed by decay,
And power moves from land to land.

Now the pigeons make their home,
Where rafters rot and doors stand open;
Wrenched off and leaning, windows broken,
We will stand, until the day
The council bulldoze us away…'

And yet, the spring shoots did push up,
Through autumn's dead leaves bringing green;
And when our homes were cleared away,
Growth did follow on decay:

Tessa Sanderson Place
Daley Thompson Way—
Housing neat
For work and play,
On Google maps, it's there today
Between the Silverthorne and Queenstown Roads—
Names I love, once my abode.

Italian interlude

Palinuro/Tavarnelle/Catania

On a silent hillside,
We sit so quietly
In a distant dreamlike world
Beneath the olive trees.

Stars pop out like mushrooms,
Sun goes down in gold;
Lighthouse beams and vivid dreams
Throughout the night unfold.

Spring slides into summer
Around the end of May,
Fireflies by evening
Swallows fly by day.

Down by the fish market
They're hosing down the streets;
Underneath a shabby arcade
A hobo sits in the heat

Of a fire he's scraped together
From a couple of garbage cans…
It's just the way things happen
In this poor but vibrant land.

Madras '89

If the goodness of your hearts my friends was seen in worldly wealth,
The streets and alleys of Madras would now be paved with gold;
If the story of your kindnesses was woven from your lives,
It would warm the heart wherever it was told.

When I saw your palm thatch shanties with their bravely flying flags,
They spoke to me of self-esteem and pride;
Disease the mortal enemy from rank and stinking pools,
But the dwellings there were neat and clean inside.

We went to see the tailor to be measured up for clothes
And went back for a fitting ten days on…
The young man had a long face for we all had lost a friend,
The clothes were there – the kind old man was gone.

The statues of your heroes are placed along the shore—
Gandhi, Avviyaar and Bardhiyar;
Your people love and honour their commitment to the truth,
To the ideal beside the fact of what things are.

In the gardens of Theosophy the light plays on the ground,
And the leaves are lit translucent by the sun;
There breathes a fine serenity a calm and timeless peace,
A spirit in which all can live as one.
Sun went down behind the palm trees and rose over motorways,
Twelve hours aviation was the span!
Between an ancient culture now beginning to renew,
And a proud but sadly disunited land.

O India! Your people are still burdened in their lives
By the weight of monstrous, crushing poverty—
But there is some hope today that now the monster can be quelled,
And your struggle will be crowned with victory.

Bombay Moon

A crescent moon,
Above the high-rise buildings of Bombay;
Those eve-of-travel sharp reflections,
Now the mind will stray.

Not far from here the gate is standing,
Where the travellers made their way;
Some as conquerors, some as pilgrims,
Intent on changing night to day.

Or fearful of a wrathful imam,
Whose bloody sword betrayed his creed;
Spurred by gold, spurred by glory,
Each explorer had his need.

In fact the ladies came this distance,
From the isle of worldly power…
Brought to make a fine alliance,
A soldier in an Orient bower.

Arabs, Portuguese and English,
Brought their spirits to this shore;
For good or ill they lived or perished,
Bringing order, bringing war.

Passion fills the daily landscape,
In the earth and in the air:
A hidden force that stirred and beckoned—
India's heartbeat…..

Seringapatam

Where Wellington and Tipu fought
I slept a sleep like gentle rain;
My body to a halt was brought
And sickness purged my mind and brain.

As in that trance-like state I lay
An endless flux flowed over me;
Of creeds and systems, right and wrong—
All grown from Man's ability.

Yet none of these imposed their claim
On my enforced passivity;
By that shattered strong-built fort
I felt divine uncertainty.

Iran
In this place of blue and gold
(for Omar Khayyám)

A world created in that single mind,
An antidote to loneliness and fretful care,
Flicks out droplets down the length of time,
Which come to rest where listening minds repair.

To raise the glass of wine so red and true,
And feel companionship within the sage's realm:
Both human and eternal, in wide purview,
And marked by wisdom rare in haunts of men…

Which was why Fitzgerald found his mind embraced
And held while ever working to enhance
His renderings of the Master's voice,
That came to him through choice and chance.

And Rossetti, Swinburne formed a band,
To hail that poetry's onward gift
That had emerged from desert lands,
To be honoured where the swallow and the swift

Across the world would grace the summer bright,
In a greener land, where Suffolk harvests bloomed;
And there that unsentimental mind took flight,
To become familiar in the world's own living room.

Misquoted by the powerful now,
Viewing claims of truth with ever its eyebrow raised,
With reality's onward flow at one somehow,
Admitting not that one sole name be praised.

So in this place, light blue and gold,
Where debate and friendship join to reign;
(Low gossip too no doubt, but never cold)
Let us toast the poet's name!

Pakistan

Bin Laden – a Byronic epitaph

He died a soldier at the end,
With bullets in his chest and brain;
So now he's safe in paradise—
A good result for all concerned?

India

The Ballad of Akbar and Aurangzeb

Have you heard of Akbar and Aurangzeb?
And their oh-so-different ways?
Rulers of the Moghul Empire,
In India, and surviving to this day.

Akbar he was a Sufi thinker,
Delighting in arcane philosophy;
With Hindus, Buddhists, Christians he would talk,
About the world and life's great mysteries.

Aurangzeb ruled generations later,
He murdered his brothers for the throne;
He outlawed music and performance,
And tore down Hindu temples stone by stone.

Akbar believed in freedom of religion:
Reason, said he, must be supreme;
And that hallowed region of tradition,
Should not be as a long-term prison seen.

Aurangzeb you know he was quite different -
He ordered Christian priests to be enslaved;
And what's more, he beheaded a Guru of the Sikhs,
Because Islam he refused to embrace.

Now Akbar had abolished,
The jizya tax non-Muslims had to pay;
Guess what, Aurangzeb, he re-imposed it,
So infidels were kept under his sway.

Now the future must be with Muslims like Akbar,
In our world of the coming century;
And let's hope that Aurangzebi Muslims
Can find a way to love humanity.

Have you heard of Akbar and Aurangzeb?
They're still surviving to this day.

La Ballade d'Akbar et d'Aurangzeb

Avez-vous entendu parler d'Akbar et d'Aurangzeb?
Et de leurs manières si différentes?
Empereurs aux Indes à l'époque des Moghols
- Ils existent encore à présent.

Akbar était un penseur Soufi,
Enchanté par toutes les grandes pensées;
Avec les Bouddhistes, Chrétiens, Hindous, il discutait,
Du monde et de ses grands mystères.

Aurangzeb a regné des générations plus tard,
Il a tué un frère puis de plus en plus;
Il a interdit la musique et même la danse -
Il a entièrement démoli des temples Hindous.

Akbar croyait à la liberté de la religion,
La Raison doit être le guide suprême;
Et le domaine sacrée de la tradition,
Ne doit pas être un prison à long terme.

Aurangzeb faisait complètement contraste,
Sous son règne les Chrétiens étaient asservis;
Et en plus il a décapité un gourou des Sikhs,
Parce que'il avait refusé de se convertir.

Pendant son règne Akbar avait aboli
La taxe que les infidelès devaient payer;
Par contre, Aurangzeb l'a réimposa,
Donc ils savaient qu'ils étaient dominés.

L'avenir doit être avec des gens comme Akbar,
Dans notre monde du siècle prochain;
Espérons que les adeptes d'Aurangzeb -
Commenceront à aimer leurs voisins.

Avez-vous entendu parler d'Akbar et d'Aurangzeb?
Ils existent encore à présent.

'Beatles ashram', Rishikesh, 2014

From this source of purest song,
Near where a myth-bound river flows;
In the hollows of the hills,
Came William and his bungalow.

Dear Prudence she was here,
In her quarters she did hide;
Sexy Sadie came to light,
From a trusting, then sardonic mind.

Monkeys mating in the dust—
Why don't we do it in the road?
Piggies clutching forks and knives
In their dinner clothes.

And the Queen of all the brood,
Those 'airy children of the brain';
Julia, that floating spell,
That told of loss, but also gain.

For days I stayed some miles away,
Even at that distance feeling blessed;
The landscape that I looked out on,
With wit and beauty still impressed.

Chennai 2014

Somewhere in this city is a boy whose life has changed,
Somewhere a loving mother who will never more be found;
Only three years old, he knows he'll never see her more,
For yesterday they laid her in the ground.

Let us hope that boy will now be gifted kindness as he grows,
And finds some constant caring from his own community;
Let's wish on him a loving wife and children of his own,
To make his own supporting family.

It's hard to feel that absence though that sometimes will appear,
In the morning, night, at mealtimes, or in sudden playground tears;
Can we hope it will be balanced by a type of growing strength
That will then serve to sustain him through the years?

Asian Highway

Hitching through the desert down the Asian Highway,
On the road to Afghanistan;
We were together in mind and body,
Travelling without a plan.

Travelling, travelling,
Beneath an autumn sky—
Bounded minds unravelling,
Orion way down low in the sky.

When we passed through the Indian villages
The people parted like the sea:
Grinning and pointing upwards
At the sight of my companion and me;
Hitching East with a convoy
Over the Great North Indian plain,
Preparing for a night ride
To evade the heat of the day.

Travelling, travelling,
Beneath an unfamiliar sky—
Bounded minds unravelling,
Orion moving up in the sky.

We got down before Kolkata
Where the drivers were to find their bed,
And thousands slept the streets at night
Just the pavements to cradle their heads;
They'd come in from the country
When their crops had failed out in the fields,
Then they'd sent their kids out begging
To get some kind of relief.

Unequal world we're part of it:
Shopping malls and shanty towns;

Yet I've seen a deal of progress
Since that journey over Orient ground.

Travelling, travelling,
Beneath an unfamiliar sky—
Bounded minds unravelling,
Orion rising high.

Marriage Song

Dear Nitin, Neeraja, a page has now turned,
And a new chapter opens for you
In which you will write your own story of life,
Be loving, be faithful, be true.

You have your princess, you have your prince,
With family and friends there for you—
Who all wish you right and are joined beyond sight,
By the shades of your ancestors too.

Not all can be fine and when things go awry,
Try not to prolong the upset;
But move on and break out and work out what's amiss,
So in future those things you won't get.

Look after your princess, look after your prince,
A source of both joy and delight;
To help share the load on the so-varied road,
That stretches away out of sight.

Don't think 'Black', don't think 'White'.

Don't think 'Black', think 'Unfaded',
'White' should just be 'Faded' rated;
'BAME'* is lame and bureaucratic,
A view of folk divisive, static.

After all at human dawn,
Dark skin would protect from harm;
When some moved to northern climes,
Their black pigment did decline.

Otherwise the vitamins,
Partly admitted through their skins,
Would be seriously deficient—
Isn't Nature so efficient?

Divide us not by skin colour,
Differences come from money, culture,
Not to mention geography,
Which distributes unequally.

So don't think 'Black', think 'Unfaded',
'White' should just be 'Faded' rated;
Don't resort to that word 'BAME' —
In human terms we're all the same!

*'Black, Asian and Minority Ethnic'

Afterwords II

Harder realities

9/11: Shining towers
Manchester Arena, Christchurch mosques
World at the Crossroads

And Hope is where?

The Democratic spell
The Major, his Brother,
and his never lived-with Lover
Global Rhythm
Light in the Caverns
Rock radio on the freeway

All Things Must Pass

Travelling down the road
A Spring will come

Afterwords II begins with three pieces under the title of 'Harder Realities', reflections on subsequent events. 'Shining Towers' a song lyric that records how even a little bear cub was affected by the atrocity of 9/11; next a poem written after the terrorist attacks in Manchester and New Zealand, and lastly 'World at the Crossroads' on the still-increasing difficulties posed by climate change. 'And Hope is Where?' surveys the forces that oppose those dark challenges: peoples' desire for freedom, the factor of human innovation and ingenuity, and finally the semi-mystical force of art, music and poetry. And 'All Things Must Pass' focuses on the truth of human mortality, a reminder to live in the present, 'seize the time' and appreciate the gift of life.

9/11: Shining towers

You know the day it happened, the day they seized the planes,
And brought the shining towers down in smoke and dust and flames;
Well there was a man who worked all week with victims of that day,
Who tried to soothe their troubled minds with talk, and art, and play.

Each weekend he would do his bit at an urban wildlife park,
To be with a little orphaned bear they'd put into his charge;
Now that little bear was mischievous and naughty in its play,
It would cuff him with its little paws and rush about all day.

But that weekend it was subdued: it didn't run or jump,
Or cover him with slugs or snails or sit down with a bump;
Guess what? That bear had felt the sense of sadness in his friend,
It had somehow felt that day of hate and tried to make amends

For to our friend's astonishment it came and held him tight
To offer him its sympathy and try to put things right....

You could say those acts of hatred offended Nature too,
Some spirit of benevolence awoke to heal the wound;
And it ain't too sentimental to say that Love arose:
It wakened in that little bear and in our thoughts for those

Who'd suffered on that dreadful day when all was upside down;
It rose to counter hatred and was felt throughout the town.

Manchester Arena, Christchurch mosques

Empty rooms and unused chairs,
Silence on the steps and stairs;
Works unpainted, books unread,
Stories untold, words unsaid.

From this world of vivid life,
Sent by bomb or gun or knife;
To be part of memories,
Sombre thoughts, laughter, tears.

Man-made sorrow, darkened minds,
Drawn into a state that binds
Once-free beings into hate—
Blackened seeds that germinate.

Love and nous, arms and law,
Must meet this sickness, underscore
Man's need for freedom, and defend
Such precious ideals to the end.

World at the Crossroads

There's a change in the weather,
There's a change in our lives,
That sends us journeying off
Into the night.

World at the crossroads
In the coming years;
Let's go for laughter
Let's not go for tears.

Ambition drives the human journey,
It's been biggin' up for two centuries;
Now that Mother Nature's having her say
It must be time for some new qualities....

And though Caution may not make the best of rallying cries,
And Forethought might not come naturally,
Surely these are like two new guiding stars
That now shine in our galaxy.

World at the crossroads
In the coming years;
Let's go for laughter
Let's not go for tears.

The Democratic Spell

Better the brave smiles and the tears,
Of democrats that lose the fight,
Than the cold commanding sneers,
Of rulers without oversight.

The Major, his Brother,
and his never lived-with Lover

*Inspired by 'A Very English Hero: The Making
of Frank Thompson' by Peter Conradi.*

There is a story, that when he came to die
A swirl of glowing fireflies arose before his eye;
A final gift of wonder, of gentleness and peace,
To rebuke his brutal torturers and ease his life's release.

The soldiers in the party, would say they'd aimed to miss,
When they went through his possessions, the evidence was this:
Of a man who'd loved their country, their language and their folk;
Who'd thought of nothing else but helping them to slip their yoke.

I'm thinking of his brother, the historian EP,
And how this must have changed his life – been with him constantly;
I met him once at Glastonbury, after he'd been up on stage:
An electric, rangy figure, depth and passion in his rage.

I asked him about poetry, and think I got this right,
He smiled and said he went with Blake – then disappeared from sight!
His brother was a poet too, so in the realms of verse,
He found perhaps some solace that could help the grief disperse.

And Iris Murdoch thought of him, it's guessed, when she would come to write,
On the persistence of true goodness when faced with blackest night;
So let that thought survive him, with a forerunner's refrain:
But, you know, that 'I have lived, and have not lived in vain'.

Global Rhythm

Ok, come on, tell me, 'Can you hear it?'
A rhythm a global beat,
Pulling us out of history's quicksand,
Getting us up on our feet....

People under despots, military strongmen,
Women and men, black white and brown;
People living under bullying religions,
People living in shanty towns…

They're sending up signals,
For someone to see;
They're sending up signals
'We want to be free'.

Alright come on tell me 'What are you Freedom?'
You are clothes and fire and food,
And the peoples' energies freed and harnessed,
Going on to build the common good.

You are justice and a law that is impartial,
And elections that are free and fair;
So if the rulers don't please the people,
Why, they just vanish into the air!

Well now, one day, we could be dancing,
Dancing to the global beat,
Everyone dancing together,
Everybody up on their feet.

Light in the Caverns

There are places in the natural world,
Where sunlight never falls—
In the ocean's deepest reach,
In caves beneath the moors.

But those with skill and courage,
Who carry torches bright,
Explore these darkened regions,
And make them blaze with light!

And though they soon return to night,
They can be understood;
So in a way those lights still burn,
On tape, on film, in books.

There were places in the human mix,
Beyond the reach of mind;
Where reason could not penetrate,
And the wisest eyes were blind.

But those with skill and courage,
Who weren't afraid to fight,
Explored these darkened regions,
And made them blaze with light!

In the eggshell of the skull,
There are no direct lines.
Who knows what is waiting there?
Never underestimate the human mind.

Rock radio on the freeway

Across this earth of matter,
Flows an ever-shifting sheen
Of poetry of music,
And of rhyme that can redeem

The world from repetition,
Or dull taking of Life's ways;
And heighten self-awareness,
Bringing pleasure to our days.

Wrestling with words and meaning,
Giving form to melodies;
Exerting a magnetic pull,
Are minds that make that sheen

Which is felt along the freeways,
In airports, streets and jails;
Transforming and reflecting,
The stuff of mortal days.

Travelling down the road

The slow subsiding of the flame,
Until there's just a tiny flickering,
Exists beside a turning brain,
Whose workings set one's self a-bickering.

Now there are such things as stoic balance,
Patience, goodwill, calm acceptance;
And all these things must interplay,
In face of this remorseless presence.

And co-exist with thankfulness,
For the dawning rise of each new day;
That somehow in the scheme of things
Consciousness has come one's way.

A Spring will come

For each of us will come a spring
We're destined not to see;
With fragrant flowers and new-mown grass,
And subtle scented breeze.

And yet, somehow, we will be there,
At least in loved ones' minds;
In what we've built, in what we've dreamt,
In all we've left behind.

Afterwords III

And finally – completing what has become a larger collection of mainly India-related writings - a Chennai-based children's story inspired by the 'Biscuit Bandits' who – at the time when major tunnelling works were taking place in Chennai – were terrorising the Indian rail networks and gaining considerable publicity…..

Mani Mouse and the Biscuit Bandits

CHAPTER ONE
SOMETHING MURKY AT THE STATION

It was one of the great mysteries that year in India. The disappearance of one of the massive tunnelling machines, brought in to create a subterranean Metro system in a southern Indian city, caused a great stir. How could it have happened? Who was responsible? Was the Metro jinxed?

The speculation lasted about a month, and was dying down when the vast machine reappeared just as mysteriously. Again, the press comment was feverish, but again it died down as new events and scandals unfolded. Six weeks later the incident was receding into the past. The tunneller had been recovered, the Metro was being dug, and all talk of a jinx was over. Six months down the line and the affair had been archived in peoples' minds into that rather large category of 'extraordinary things that just seem to keep on happening in India', and was, to all effect, forgotten.

Deep in his huge underground lair, Javed the Accumulator perused the morning paper and found no mention of the tunneller. Things had moved on. His early morning yawn turned into a self-satisfied smirk. Soon it would be time to put the plan into operation.

Mani mouse was feeling quite pleased with himself. He peered out of his little hiding place at all the bustle of a busy South Indian station, watching the endless flow of busy travellers making their way to and from their trains.

Yes, he thought to himself, this is a very good spot. It was just in front of a bench where people rested and ate their tiffin so there were always crumbs and sometimes bigger morsels of food for a hungry little mouse like Mani. And (he continued thinking to himself), this is a very good spot from where to start my adventures. For as his uncle Rajan always said, 'a mouse is not just a stomach', and this saying had stayed with him and perhaps encouraged his innate sense of adventure.

Last week in fact, he had travelled all the way up India's eastern coastline as far as Orissa, travelling First Class Air Conditioned with people who had the finest provisions! And at the station at Bhubaneswar, where he had rested and explored a little before returning home, he had made such good friends, including a very pretty young female mouse who he had promised to visit again. His little hiding place was perfectly positioned so that he could scuttle across to the First Class carriages when the time was right – and then he could also retreat back into a maze of tunnels if danger threatened. In which case, eventually he would find his way back to the family nest, where his wise and kindly uncle Rajan looked after his three sisters Kala, Meera and Veena. How clever he had been to find such a perfect spot!

Now approaching the bench was a family of three, a little boy and his parents, all smartly dressed with the little boy in a suit and tie. They settled down and took out their provisions. And after a few minutes they were joined by a well-dressed and obviously smart young man – soon they were all laughing together at one of his jokes.

Mani then saw the young man taking a packet of biscuits from his bag. The family all took and ate one each, the little boy dropping one in the process. 'Aha', thought Mani, 'I'll take that back to the family – they will be pleased'.

Then, as he looked, the family seemed to become drowsy. They slumped back on the bench, and went into a deep sleep. The young man, working smoothly and efficiently, then removed wallet, watch and gold ring from the father, bracelets and chains from the mother, and a gold and coral tie pin from the little boy. Then, without a backward glance, he sauntered away with his haul.

'Well something is not right there', said Mani to himself, his whiskers twitching. And then the little boy, still fast asleep, fell from the bench, grazing his arm in the fall. 'That's not good at all' said Mani. 'First that man took his little tie pin, and now this! That poor little boy will be feeling bad when he wakes up'.

Mani was glad to see a passer-by raise the alarm, and soon a crowd had gathered round the sleeping family. Then a large moustachioed policeman arrived, and solemnly stated: 'This is most certainly the work of those pesky biscuit bandits'.

After all the excitement had died down, and ambulance orderlies had taken the family for observation and rest at the government hospital, Mani pushed the biscuit that had fallen to the ground towards his hidden mouse-hole, and let it roll right down the series of tunnels that led to his family's quarters.

'That policeman was silly not to notice it', he thought as he followed. 'It would have been valuable evidence, and I'm sure, they could have got some clues from it'. And then a great and inspiring thought came to him: 'If the police cannot solve this case, then I, Mani mouse, will have to track them down'.

At that moment, he arrived in the central room of his family's home. The biscuit had rolled into the middle of the room and was being eyed hungrily by his three sisters. 'Don't touch it!' shouted Mani, 'I believe that biscuit is drugged!'

'But how can we tell?' asked Kala, the eldest of the sisters. At that point Uncle Rajan spoke up. 'I suggest we take it to cockroach corner', he said, 'and see what happens to it'.

So they pushed it to the intersection of the many underground tunnels that was the favourite meeting point of their cockroach neighbours. A couple of hours later they returned to see a most curious sight. The biscuit had gone, and round about, lying on their backs, twitching their little legs from time to time and as fast asleep as it is possible to be, were their cockroach neighbours of the underground colony. What deeply impressed the mouse family, was that they were all snoring loudly.

'Well that settles that' said Mani confidently when they had returned to their home. 'The policeman said there were biscuit bandits on the loose, and I do believe he was right'. There was a pause, and then he said grandly 'And *I* am going to do something about it'.

'You mean, *we*' said Uncle Rajan, Kala, Veena and Meera in unison. Then they sang a made-up mouse song together:

'By your side you know we'll be:
Uncle wise and sisters three;
Though we're small, no brains we lack,
By jingo, yes! This case we'll crack!'

Well, Mani felt very cheered by this show of family support, and they settled down for a council of war. How on earth were they going to tackle the biscuit bandits? They all agreed that the first priority was reconnaissance, trying to find out more about the mysterious gang, and then making a proper plan.

CHAPTER TWO
INSIDE THE BISCUIT BANDITS'
HEADQUARTERS

Chattabhai the Cunning approached Javed the Accumulator in his underground lair.

'Sir, good news' he said, 'Tamil Nadu section is about to report'

And with that the receiving hatch in the ceiling opened, and down a chute into a padded steel container poured a cornucopia of rings, watches, bracelets, gold chains, wallets stuffed with rupee notes and expensive-looking children's toys.

You might have thought Javed's heart would have softened a bit at the thought of robbing a child of its happiness, but not a bit of it.

'Oho!' he said, 'Oho!' 'Very good, and those toys will fetch a good price. See the Tamil Nadu branch get their bonus, Chattabhai'.

It was in this way that he maintained the loyalty of his staff. In addition to a very fair monthly salary, he also saw that their children got to go to school, and that bonuses for excellent work were paid.

Now he clapped his hands: 'Gold squad, gold squad!' he shouted, and two operatives moved as one towards the newly received hoard. Working silently and efficiently they sorted through the haul, and soon had extracted a pile of gold jewellery. This they took back to their area of the underground HQ, laid it on a table, and, while one stoked up a furnace, the other separated any jewels from the gold. Soon it was all melted down and poured into five ounce moulds. The bars were then stamped 'South African gold' because Javed had said this would fool the police.

Then they reported back to Javed sitting on his impressive throne. 'Three bars, sir, this time'.

Javed calculated rapidly. 15 ounces in total, gold at $2,000 an ounce that was $30,000 in total! Not at all bad. And Andhra section was due to report in the next day. They *were* doing well.

He clapped his hands again: 'Banking section' he barked, and another two employees stepped forward to count all the money in the pile.

And so life continued in the headquarters of the All India Association of Biscuit Bandits. It was cleverly concealed behind high screens constructed from bamboo poles and woven palm leaf screens, and stood alongside the busy road outside the city known as the East Coast Road, or ECR for short. Inside the screened-off area was a small temporary looking building; this was where the bandits would report, and deposit their takings. They would open the hatch, and down into Javed's headquarters would slide their takings for the month. Sometimes, curious, they would peer down to try to glimpse its workings: it seemed huge, with uniformed staff buzzing around on little electric trolleys, or huddled over desks making up accounts, or calculating salaries. Once they even saw Javed himself, seated on a splendid red and gold chair, gently stroking a little white cat that all villains of his type had to have if they were to be considered true and proper scary gangsters of the worst type.

Then they would depart to resume their biscuit bandit activities, properly impressed by the sheer organisation of the group they called 'the company'. Passing out of the side entrance they would pass the large sign that fronted onto the road – 'The All India Association of Bread Bakers (AIABB)' it read. How they would laugh! 'What a clever fellow Mr Javed is' they would say. It really was the AIABB, but not in the way everybody would think. 'Our boss is the master of deception' they would reflect, and this would send them on their way in good spirits, ready for their next crime spree.

Of course, both the railway authorities and the police were getting concerned at the rising levels of theft from passengers in the railway stations and on the trains themselves. And it seemed to be a national epidemic! From Punjab to Orissa, from Assam to Tamil Nadu, complaints and reported thefts were rising dramatically. Naturally they responded with a warning video on the television monitors installed in stations, but they were no match for the biscuit bandits' media skills.

For Chattabhai concocted an advertising campaign that ran on TVs in every state
when the biscuit bandits realised that the warnings were beginning to have an
effect on their takings. It had such an effective jingle, with winning words
written by Chattabhai and such catchy music by the HQ's resident musician that
it neutralized the official campaign. Chattabhai's song went like this:

'When you're hungry on the train,
Your rumbling tum will give you pain.
You know what would a difference make?
Doughnuts, muffins, biscuits, cake'

It aroused no suspicion, because Chattabhai realised that including biscuits with
other bakery items would throw investigators off the trail. And on the ground, as
the bandits went about their work, they found that nearly everyone had seen the
ad, even singing the last two lines with a smile as they would accept a drugged
biscuit. Such is the power of advertising, the cheery jingle swept all before it,
and the authorities were powerless to stop the relentless rise in thefts. It seemed
that nothing could halt the rise and rise of the biscuit bandits.

CHAPTER THREE
FINDING OUT MORE

The huge express train, watched carefully by three little mice hiding in the shadows, had just pulled into the station. It was 05.00 in the morning, and from the carriages a veritable torrent of passengers disembarked, heading for the station exit laden with suitcases, bags and parcels. Having travelled from a textile town around seven hours away on the train, they were now returning to their families in the big city for the weekend.

Finally, the flow came to an end, and, from the goods carriages the train's freight started to be disembarked. Veera, Meena and Kala watched carefully. They were waiting for the morning papers as part of the reconnaissance mission recommended by Uncle Rajan.

But first they had to wait as Ismael the vegetable man loaded fresh produce from the hills onto his distinctive van. Painted with cauliflowers, carrots, potatoes and lettuces it was well known to all the mouse family and, it was so regular in the times of its visits, they often used it to check the time of day.

After he had left, they watched as the newsvendor pasted up the headline news outside his stand, and then scurried back to their nest to pass on the information they had gathered. They were shocked by what they had read: 'NOW BISCUITS BANDITS ROB CHILD IN GUJARAT'.

'Gujarat' said Mani thoughtfully, as the family gathered to digest the news. That means that 13 states have now been affected'.

'It must be quite an operation' said Meera, 'I bet there's a bandit queen directing it' said Veena, 'and *I* think we have to find their headquarters' said Kala.

At which point, the little family of mice became despondent. Find their headquarters indeed – why, it could be anywhere in India! Even wise Uncle Rajan had nothing to say. All Mani's big plans to solve the case and bring the bandits to justice seemed like a dream that could never come true.

The three sisters curled up together and drifted off to sleep. Wise Uncle Rajan retired to meditate in his special chamber. And Mani was left all alone, with the burden of his dreams weighing him down, feeling foolish at his overblown ambitions.

'Perhaps this has always been my trouble' he thought to himself. 'I always have these big dreams, but never manage to carry them out. If only I could manage to be a mouse of reasonable ambitions' he sighed, 'just interested in food and family'.

But then, one of Uncle Rajan's sayings came into his head, that he had learnt (so Uncle Rajan said) from a Chinese mouse who once had landed in the port. The two had had many philosophical discussions, and Uncle Rajan would often repeat afterwards something the Chinese mouse had said – 'A journey of a thousand miles begins with a single step'.

'That is very true' thought Mani, 'and anything is better than sitting here feeling sorry for myself. I'm going back up to the station to see what I can see'. And he remembered another of his Uncle's sayings: 'From small openings come major opportunities', and so he set off purposefully up the tunnels that led to the station platforms.

For an hour he watched from his favourite spot, hoping that something, anything would turn up. His heart was beginning to sink as the time passed, but then he spotted the same smartly dressed young man, the original biscuit bandit, coming towards the bench. The young man had spotted a family of four resting there, and as before offered them biscuits and then relieved them of their valuables, placing them in a collecting bag he carried over his shoulder.

'Now's my chance!' thought Mani with a sudden rush of blood, and before the thief could zip up his bag he jumped right in, finding himself alongside a true hoard of treasure: gold chains, rings and bracelets, watches, rupee notes, and wallets bulging with credit cards. Then the zip was closed, and Mani found himself in the darkness, suddenly aware that he was now facing a journey into the unknown. 'I might as well make myself comfortable' he thought, and found a comfy spot between a soft leather wallet and a silk scarf the bandit had robbed. 'Ooh, it's as good as my little spot at home' he was thinking, when the bag was lifted suddenly, then swaying from side to side as the biscuit bandit headed towards the station exit.

There an expensive-looking car was waiting for him in the premium parking spaces outside the station, and soon Mani was surrounded by unfamiliar noises – the changing note of a car's engine, car horns, the shouts of traffic policemen, and the conversation and laughter in the back of the car. 'They seem very pleased with their ill-gotten gains,' thought Mani, 'but I intend to wipe the smiles from their faces'.

It took over an hour to reach the outskirts of the city. Now the constant stop-start of the car changed to a steadier note as it reached the new section of road at the beginning of the ECR. Then they travelled for another half hour before Mani felt the car slowing, and finally turning onto a rough track. He heard a gate being opened, and then was bumped up and down as the car made its way over rough ground.

Suddenly, things happened very quickly. There was a harsh metallic scraping sound (the delivery shute being opened), shouts from below ('Tamil Nadu section reporting'), the bag's zip being roughly opened, and then a frightening slide downwards with Mani instinctively curling into a ball to protect himself. Then Mani and the contents of the bag came to a halt. He looked around himself. He seemed to be in a large open box – before he had time to think there was a loud call: 'Gold squad, gold squad!' and soon two pairs of hands were rummaging through the box, finding all the valuable gold that had been stolen.

'I've got to get out of here', thought Mani, and scampered up one of the man's shirtsleeves as he reached in. 'Aaargh!' went the man as Mani ran up his arm, and reaching his shoulder, jumped into the unknown. 'What is it?' asked Javed from his seat. 'Mouse, sir, little mouse' he shouted, 'how did it get here?'

Javed's cat, scenting a mouse, bared its teeth and hissed. 'Never mind' said Javed, 'my little princess here can have some fun later'.

And so Mani penetrated the headquarters of the biscuit bandits. But what was he to do now?

CHAPTER FOUR
OF MICE AND MEN

The night before Mani's expedition, Chief Inspector Rahul Sabir had had a dream or rather a flash of understanding that he thought might provide a clue in the long-running case of the biscuit bandits. For three months now he had been working with a crack team of detectives on the case, but had got nowhere. Well, not quite nowhere, for they had recovered at stations across India three of the wrappers used by the bandits, each of which had an individual red sticker, presumably to show that the biscuits it contained had been drugged.

He needed to come up with some results soon: not only had most of India's states been affected, but foreign travellers had been targeted too. He had been shown some of the headlines in newspapers from abroad: 'Phantom bandits plague Indian Railways'; 'Drugged biscuits cause mayhem on Indian trains'. Questions had been raised in Parliament, further adding to the pressure on him.

Now he looked out at his ten-strong team of detectives assembled in the operations room. 'Ladies and gentleman' he began. 'I firmly believe that police work largely depends on carrying out tried and trusted routine traditional procedures. However', he continued, 'we must also be ready to admit the flame of inspiration into our work.'

At this point his detectives exchanged glances as if to say 'Here goes the boss again'.

'Last night' he continued, 'I was sitting with my good wife watching the latest episode of our favourite soap opera. In the commercial break, as usual, they showed that confoundedly catchy advertisement for bakery products. After retiring to bed the tune kept going round and round my head, and that night I had a most unusual dream. My dream was …' he paused for a second, 'I dreamed I was travelling on a train made entirely of biscuits!'

The detectives all burst out laughing – they could not help it, even though he was their boss.

'Ah, well', said the Chief Inspector, 'you may well laugh, but I believe' he continued, 'that my dream was telling me that the key words in that confounded advertisement were 'train' and 'biscuit'. In other words, I believe we will find that the advertisement was produced by the bandits to encourage the consumption of biscuits on our trains, thereby making their work so much easier'.

'By Jove Sir!' exclaimed the keenest of the detectives, Lakshmi, springing to her feet and saluting, 'I do believe you've got it Sir!'

'Thank you detective' replied Sabir, 'for your confidence in my dreaming method. I may write a book about it one day. But now comes the application of our old-fashioned policing methods to my moment of inspiration. I want you to find out exactly who placed this advertisement, and see if you can trace them. I suspect we may be on the trail of a national gang of goondas. So be careful, and good luck!'

And, with that, the detectives fanned out across the city to begin their work.

Mani's little whiskers moved excitedly as he looked out at the biscuit bandits' HQ. It was a huge underground cavern, humming with activity, all orchestrated by a sinister-looking man with a moustache sitting on a red and gold chair. Mani paid special attention to the small white cat he was petting, but decided it would pose little danger.

'I'm sure it's too well-fed and pampered to pay any attention to a little mouse like me' he thought to himself. So he decided to begin the next part of the mission, a thorough investigation of the bandits' base.

Creeping carefully along he came to what looked like the most important part of the operation – the manufacture of the drugged biscuits. Two chemists in white coats were carefully using a syringe to place a droplet of liquid on each biscuit. Then the two other workers would carefully put the biscuits back into the original packaging and place a small red sticker on the packet to show that it had been treated. Shelves on the wall were filling with packets that would then be distributed to the different sections of the organisation.

Then there was a room marked 'Training and media'. Mani did not know what this was – so he passed on to the next room – 'Banking and Finance'. There a distinguished-looking older man was counting money and registering stolen credit cards on a computer. Then there was a little furnace being stoked up for the day's takings of gold. Mani saw the rings and bracelets being placed in a little round container and then melted down over the flame.

And finally, in pride of place, illuminated by little spotlights so that Javed could always see his treasure trove, was the collection of gold bars, stacked high and growing month by month. Mani looked up at the pile in awe – so this was the bandits' treasure!

Suddenly, he was knocked on his back and held to the ground by sharp claws. He found himself looking up at the face he sometimes would see in his worst nightmares – the face of a cat, its teeth bared. 'Got you' hissed Princess, Javed's white cat. 'Come to steal our treasure, have you? Well I'll make short work of you'.

Now there is a phrase in English which people sometimes use to show how annoyed they are. 'I kicked the cat' they will say; 'When I lost my job I went home and kicked the cat!' Usually they haven't actually kicked anything – it's just an expression – but on this occasion, unfortunately for Princess, it really happened.

For young Ganesh, who had been hired by the bandits to clean up their base and act as an occasional driver, had just had a blazing row with Javed himself. Javed was furious that Ganesh had answered back when he had ticked him off for not keeping the electric trolleys clean enough, and had told him – 'One more bit of bad work, and you're out!'

So Ganesh was in a bad mood, and very cross with Javed too. So, when he saw his boss's cat Princess right in his path he could not restrain himself. He drew back his right leg (luckily for Princess he was barefoot) and aimed a tremendous kick in her direction. An astonished Princess sailed through the air, landing in a heap in front of the gold bars. Mani, miraculously saved, scurried off into the shadows. Meanwhile Ganesh found himself being firmly held by the ear. 'Right' said Vadhabhai the Violent, 'I'm taking you to the boss'.

Minutes later Ganesh was being roughly ejected from the base. Seeing his opportunity to escape, Mani scuttled through the open door into the sunlight. 'I've seen enough' he said to himself, 'now I've got to get back and tell the others'.

CHAPTER FIVE
TIGHTENING THE NET

Mani scurried after Ganesh as he made his way to the East Coast Road. It was built up with little shops and lodges, and the traffic was building up as the sun rose over the sea. Having lost his job Ganesh had decided to get roaring drunk at a little lodge he knew. Mani was intent on somehow getting back to his family at Central Station. But how? The journey out had seemed an awfully long way, and there were no trains out here he could hitch a ride on.

As he made his way along the mud track, out of the corner of his eye, he saw an elephant being led out by its mahout for its morning bath. However, he paid it little attention, preoccupied as he was with getting home.

In the event he was in luck, because as he reached the roadside, he saw to his left a familiar looking vehicle parked by a newly built restaurant. It was Ismael the vegetable man's van, the one that drove up the station platform early every morning to collect the vegetables that had been grown in the hills. 'There's my lift home,' thought Mani, and he climbed in and hid himself in the back under some sacking.

'Ismael' he heard a voice saying, 'I want my vegetables early in the morning, as early as you can do'

'Yes chief,' replied Ismael. 'The train comes in at 5.45 a.m. prompt., it takes me about 45 minutes to load up – I should be here by 7.30. That's no problem chief,' he said; 'every day I will see you' And he jumped in and started the engine, heading off to collect another load from the late morning train.

Back in the family home, Mani was greeted with some relief by his family. His sisters clustered round – 'Are you alright?' they squeaked, 'we've been so worried. A whole day and a night you've been gone'.

And then Uncle Rajan came out. 'Well Mani' he said, 'What have you discovered?'

And so, Mani told them the whole story of how he'd discovered the headquarters of the biscuit bandits, how there was a big pile of gold bars, and how a very frightening cat called Princess had almost got him. And he told them about Javed the Accumulator who seemed to be the boss, and how there was a goonda called Vadhabhai the Violent who was in charge of security. And how he had escaped, and how they could use the vegetable van to travel between the station and the biscuit bandits' hideout.

'Very good' said Uncle Rajan, 'you have done well. Is that absolutely everything though? Is there anything else you can remember?'

Mani was silent, thinking back. 'Oh yes' he said finally, 'As I was escaping, I saw in the next compound an elephant coming out for its bath'.

'An elephant?' said Uncle Rajan. 'Leave it to me. We'll need two or three days of surveillance, and then we'll strike!'

At the Central police station, the detectives were gathering to make their morning report to Inspector Sabir. As he entered the room they stood to attention and saluted.

'Now then detectives' he said, 'what have you discovered? Has my dream given us the vital clue we needed?'

Well, sorry Sir, but actually – no, they replied. It turned out, they said, that the advertisement was genuine. The advertising agency had all the documentation, and confirmed that it had been booked and paid for by the All India Association of Bread Bakers – The AIABB. There was an address on the East Coast Road, and a detective confirmed that the Association was based there. At least, he said, there was big sign with the Association name on the palm hoardings.

'And did you actually see inside?' asked Inspector Sabir.

There was silence. And then the youngest and keenest detective, Lakshmi, spoke up.

'Sir, there was something a little odd about the payment'.

'Really?' said Sabir, 'and what was that?'

'Well sir, they paid not by cash or cheque but …. with a gold bar. Of South African origin too'.

'Ah yes' said Sabir, 'a gold bar. Paid in by the All Indian Association of Bread Bakers, or AIABB. Don't you see detectives, someone is having a laugh at our expense. Trying to run rings round us, assuming we're not very bright? Well they've run up against the wrong man, because' … and here his voice rose dramatically, and he banged his fist on the table – 'Chief Inspector Sabir is on the case!'

'And his team of crack detectives' said one of them from the back.

'Well if you're so sharp', said Sabir, 'does anything strike you as odd about the so-called All Indian Association of Bread Bakers – or - (he laid a heavy stress on the last two letters) the AIA*BB*?'

'Of course,' said Lakshmi, 'the All India Association of Biscuit Bandits. It all makes sense. Gosh they're cheeky – well we'll show them'.

And then the door flew open, and in stepped Sabir's deputy. 'Sir, there's been an arrest!' he blurted out. 'Down on the East Coast Road, an associate of the biscuit bandits called Ganesh – and he's singing like a bird! Drunk as a lord on feni he was. He's told us everything, they've got an underground headquarters with gold and everything – they run the whole thing from there! On the East Coast Road – who could believe it?'

'Right' said Sabir, 'We'll need two or three days of surveillance, and then we'll strike!''

Now there has been one great mystery so far in this story, and that has been how the huge tunnelling machine used for the city Metro came to be used to dig out the biscuit bandits' headquarters. But there is another mystery too - how Uncle Rajan came to have a secret understanding with elephants.

It is well known that elephants have an irrational fear of mice, but something had happened long ago that had given Uncle Rajan a great advantage in life – the ability to ask elephants to do things that he wanted them to. Maybe something had happened like in that famous story when a hermit living in the desert had come across a lion in agonizing pain, and had removed a horrible thorn from its paw. Later, that story went on, the hermit was taken to the mighty Colosseum in the city of Rome to be fed to the lions because he didn't believe in Roman gods like Jupiter or Mars. As the gateway opened, and out rushed a mighty lion to gobble him up, the hermit closed his eyes, not wanting to look at the terrifying (and very hungry) animal rushing up to him. But guess what? Instead of teeth and claws sinking into him he felt his face being gently licked, and he opened his eyes to see the very lion he had helped sitting beside him, tame as a gentle kitten, protecting him from any harm that might come to him... And all because he had helped that very lion back in the desert.

Something like that could have happened long ago in Uncle Rajan's past. Perhaps he had knawed through an imprisoning rope, stopped someone hurting an elephant, or bit a hunter suddenly to stop him shooting. But from somewhere, somehow, he had got the secret of talking to elephants in a way that made them trust him and know they should try to help. Imagine what he could have done! 'Break down that bank door, would you please?' – or – 'could you tread on that annoying mongoose for me?' But wise Uncle Rajan knew that with great power came great responsibility, and in fact he had only used his power once before.

Now, he told Mani and his sisters, the time had come for his powers to be used again. 'I will go down on the vegetable van' he said, 'and make contact with our elephant friend. You see us mice are rather small, and so it can be difficult for us, but with an elephant on our side we could cause a bit of a commotion. I will be back as soon as possible – and you, make a plan for when we have broken down the bandits' door.'

And so Mani, Veera, Meena and Kala huddled together after Uncle Rajan had left, thinking of how they could bring the bandits down. The more they thought about it, the more difficult it seemed. And there was Princess to contend with, not to mention Vadhabhai the Violent. It was a lot for little mice to do, but Mani fired everybody up with his enthusiasm for the task.

CHAPTER SIX
THE RAID(S)

At last, the big day dawned. Mani, Veera, Meera, Kala and Uncle Rajan had set the time of their attack for 8.00 in the morning, soon after they had arrived on the vegetable van. Uncle Rajan had talked to the elephant whose name was Oscar, and agreed a plan with him. Inspector Sabir and his detectives had set the time of *their* attack for 8.15, and had appeared on the East Coast Road outside the compound in different disguises.

In the biscuit bandits' headquarters meanwhile, unaware of the developments that were taking place, Javed had laid on a lavish breakfast, as he always did for his employees. There were dosai, idli, vadai, coconut and tomato chutney, and two types of sambhar. And steaming tea and coffee of course—all served by a smiling chef in his spotless white uniform, from stainless steel tureens kept hot by paraffin flames.

Javed was eating with his employees from the gold and banking squads, flanked by Vadhabhai and Chattabhai. 'How are your children doing?' he was asking. 'Oh yes sir, very well. They are doing well at school and your help means so much to our family sir'.

Javed looked across the cavernous underground chamber at his stack of gold bars under their bright lights. It was funny, recently he had been thinking, well, somehow those gold bars seemed to be losing their appeal. You can't eat them after all, and they just sit there and no nothing. In fact, he was beginning to find that he got much more satisfaction from listening to his workers' stories of how their children were making progress at school, and growing up fit and healthy.

Perhaps he was losing his hunger for his job as leader of the biscuit bandits. Then Chattabhai leaned across the table. 'Mr Javed Sir' he said, 'Punjab section is to report today. And they tell me they have a massive haul'.

At that moment there was a huge trumpeting noise from outside. And then a mighty crash as the door at the top of the ramp shivered on its foundations. Another mighty trumpeting, another crash, and then the door fell to the ground.

The sunlight flooded in, and the astonished bandits looked up from their table to see Oscar the elephant framed in the doorway.

'We're under attack!' shouted Javed, 'Vadhabhai, VADHABHAI!'

Vadhabhai rushed forward with a thick bamboo pole ready to attack the massive elephant. 'That man doesn't have an ounce of fear in his whole body' thought Javed. But then they saw Oscar slowly retreat up the ramp.

'What's going on, he can't be frightened of us', said Chattabhai. 'There must be a secondary force coming in'.

Then, as Vadhabhai stood in the broken gateway with the sunlight streaming in, that secondary force appeared at the top of the ramp. Framed in the sunlight, standing proud to take on wrongdoing and make the world a better place – it was Mani, Veera, Meena and Kala.

The biscuit bandits of course, fell about laughing at their table. 'Ha!' they laughed, and Javed clapped his hands for Princess. The mouse force scattered as Princess ran towards them, but Mani was not quick enough. Princess pounced on him and pinned him to the floor. 'You again' she hissed, 'I hope you've got a Plan B '.

'Come on' squeaked Kala, 'let's get that cat!' And with that, the battling sisters ignored all their mouse knowledge, which was of course to avoid cats at all costs, and leapt on Princess – tickling and biting her to try and make her let Mani go. As they held on, grimly aware that now it was a matter of do or die, they heard Oscar trumpeting wildly outside, trying to attract attention.

And it was at that point that Inspector Sabir and his team of detectives appeared, right on time, just as Uncle Rajan had predicted. 'You see', he had told his young relatives, 'we are only small mice, but if I can get Oscar to kick up a huge racket, someone is bound to call the police, and then we will have got them'.

And so, it seemed, it had turned out. The police all ran down the ramp into the bandits' lair through the shattered door, blowing their whistles and shouting. Detective Lakshmi scooped up a white cat that was writhing on the ground to protect it from being trampled, letting Mani and his sisters escape. They watched as the police rounded up the gang. Chattabhai the Cunning lived up to his name by pretending to be an undercover policeman. 'At last you've arrived' he said, 'I was worried you'd never get here'.

Chief Inspector Sabir put him in handcuffs anyway; he had come across the same trick before. Vadhabhai the Violent picked up his bamboo pole and ran at the police, but was tripped up by something unseen, which could have been a little mouse. He too found himself in irons.

The gold squad, the chemists and the accountant were all too timid to put up a fight, and that just left Javed the Accumulator, the mighty boss of the biscuit bandits. But all the fight had gone out of him too. He just had one request to make. 'Please sir, can we have a group photo - *please*? I would like to show it to my grandchildren'.

'Alright' said Chief Inspector Sabir, 'It will look good on the police station wall too'. And so the detectives sat Javed down in his red and gold chair, and gathered round to pose for the photograph.

'Come on' squeaked Mani, 'we must be in it too' and the whole mouse family ran out to the front where they were snapped standing on their hind legs at the front.

As the bandits were led away in handcuffs, and Princess was placed, now hissing more furiously than ever, in a cage kindly provided by the Maneka Gandhi Institute for Animal Welfare, Mani, Veera, Meena, Kala and Uncle Rajan joined forces by Oscar's elephant house outside.

'Bye Oscar!' said Uncle Rajan, 'thanks for your help'.

Oscar lifted his head and trumpeted wildly. To be honest, it had been a welcome break from his daily routine, and he had enjoyed breaking down that strong wooden door.

And finally, the little mouse family reflected on their success as they bumped their way back home in the vegetable van.

'I think this could be a blueprint' said Mani.

'For what?' asked Veena.

'To show what mice can do, of course'.

And with that thought, they returned home and had a well-deserved rest from their labours.

CHAPTER SEVEN
AND FINALLY......

Javed the Accumulator, Vadhabhai and Chattabhai were seated on the hard wooden bench, uncomfortable in their handcuffs, and flanked by other members of their team – the gold squad, the banking section, the chemists who had drugged the biscuits and the elderly accountant whose name was Mr Manikanda. Also with them were the two representatives of the Punjab section who had walked right into the police raid and had been nabbed on the spot.

Behind them the police were erecting their infamous sign – 'All India Association of Bread Bakers (AIABB)'. After all the trouble the biscuit bandits had caused, they were going to make sure their success in arresting them got some attention. So they were arranging a major press conference. It was going to be the news photo of the day.

'Pride comes before a fall, eh boss?' said Chattabhai ruefully, as their sign which had caused them such amusement was raised behind them. 'You know, Chattabhai', replied Javed, 'It reminds me of that song- 'I fought the law – and the law won'.

At that moment the double doors that led into the room were opened and a stream of journalists and photographers rushed in, eager to get the best places at the press conference. They had already been shown around the Biscuit Bandits' headquarters, and the organisation and scale of the operation had created massive interest around the country – and beyond.

'James Bond-type villains nabbed in police raids' read one headline. 'Biscuit boss modelled himself on film villains' read another. This was due to their discovery of Princess, the white cat that had caught their imagination. There were so many photographs of Princess taken that eventually an animal rights group went to court and stopped them. So many photographs, they said, were violating the privacy of an innocent animal.

Now Chief Inspector Sabir stepped forward. 'Ladies and gentlemen of the press' he said. 'Before you are the mighty Biscuit Bandits now brought low by India's vigilant enforcers of the law. For over two years they have terrorised the country, robbing families and causing mayhem. Now they are under lock and key, the place we know they ought to be. Do you have any questions?'

'Sir, sir, I worked on the story of the missing Metro tunneller over two years ago. There has never been a satisfactory explanation, but have recent events thrown any light on the matter?'

'Aha' said Chief Inpector Sabir wisely, 'indeed they have. During my interrogation of Chattabhai the Cunning – this is how he was known to the gang – I obtained a full explanation of the mystery'.

And here he turned to Chattabhai. 'Tell the public what you told me – if you cooperate things will be better for you'.

And so Chattabhai stood and faced the press. 'It was I, Chattabhai, who did the Metro tunneller job. It took two gold bars, but for that I got a helicopter to lift it off during the monsoon. It was a dark dark night, pouring with rain - no one could hear a thing! It was delivered to our base, and we got cracking on the digging. Took a whole month, but the boss was real pleased with the result. Then it went back the same way'.

He sat down, half expecting a round of applause.

Another journalist stood up. 'Sir, I believe that somehow the elephant in the neighbouring compound had a role in this operation. Was this planned?'

'No' said the Chief Inspector. 'And this remains one of the continuing mysteries about this case. There is no doubt that this elephant, Oscar by name, broke down the main door. And the trumpeting he made caused us to bring forward our operation. Naturally I questioned his mahout, and found out that that morning he was proceeding peacefully to have his bath, when he suddenly stopped, sank to his knees, and put his ear to the ground. The mahout said it was as if he was listening to some tiny voice, and then – he went berserk!

He threw his head back, trumpeted madly like he was going into battle, and charged into the neighbouring compound. Where the bandits were, of course. And then he found their main gate, and shattered it into pieces. And all the time making such a huge noise that we had to bring our operation forward. I've never seen anything like it before'.

Detective Lakshmi stepped forward. 'That's all the questions for now' she said. 'The court case will open in two weeks' time. I'm sure you'll all be there'.

Mr Justice Tata looked down on the forlorn group of biscuit bandits sitting in the dock of the court. In front of them were the stacked gold bars from their hideout, clear evidence of their wrongdoing. And indeed, the jury had taken hardly any time to find them all guilty.

And then sentence had been passed. There was no doubt that the offences were extremely serious, and the prison sentences had to reflect that. No wonder the biscuit bandits were looking glum.

But Mr Justice Tata had something up his sleeve. He loved his country, and he often thought, as major criminal cases passed through his court, what a pity the whole thing was. He could usually see that the wrongdoers actually had a lot of talent, it was just that it had gone off in the wrong direction – like a skew-whiff rocket. Now if those skills could be properly directed, well, everyone would benefit, including the country. So he would look very carefully, as each case unfolded, for signs of those skills that he thought could be harnessed for good.

'This has been a most serious case', he told the bandits, beginning his final comments after sentencing. 'And the sentences passed have been appropriate. But I have to tell you all, as this case has progressed, that I have found you to be, in your own way – a way which of course I must strongly condemn – really quite clever fellows'.

The bandits looked up, surprised. What was going on?

'And also, not without your own moral code. For example, we heard about the ejection of Ganesh from your headquarters after he had kicked Princess the cat. And we also heard that Mr Manikanda the accountant saw that he received all his back pay before he was thrown out. This of course, enabled him to get seriously drunk outside and led him give away the location of your den'.

'But, Mr Manikanda' – and here he addressed the elderly accountant, 'Your accountancy work for the bandits was found to be excellent, careful and scrupulous indeed. And so, I am convinced that if you just find the right place

for yourself you can do something for everyone's good. I am directing that
one third of your sentence will be spent in the community, trying to improve
the accounts of schools in difficulties'.

Now he turned to the gold squad. 'You two' said Mr Justice Tata, 'have been
responsible for producing the gold bars we see in front of us. Everyone in this
court', he continued, 'can see the care and skill you have taken. Each bar is a
work of craftsmanship, and has been found to weigh exactly the right amount.
I cannot see why your talents cannot find a better use. And so I am directing
that a third of *your* sentences shall be spent at a local university, studying the
science of metals. And after that, with a proper qualification, you should be
able to work in all kinds of different fields'.

'And that also goes for you two' continued the judge, looking down at the two
chemists who had drugged all the biscuits used by the bandits. 'Your offence
was most serious, for it is a great crime to administer drugs against someone's
will. The only thing I can see in your favour is that we did not see the kind of
tragedies that could have happened if you had been less skilled. But you must
put your skills to better use, and so I am directing that you spend one third of
your sentence working with a company that develops medicines to combat
malaria'.

Mr Justice Tata then turned to Vadhabhai. 'Your name was Vadhabai the
Violent' he said, 'and you were the chief enforcer for the bandits. Brute force
is never an attractive thing, but the events in the case showed you to be capable
of great bravery. Indeed, we heard how you were even willing to take on an
elephant that appeared to be going rogue. Such courage is unusual, and should
be used in the service of our country. And so I direct that one third of your
sentence shall be split between time in an army training camp, and time
working as a boxing coach with our young people. One of those professions
could be right for you'.

'Now, Chattabhai' said Mr Justice Tata, 'there is no doubt that you were the
brains behind the bandits. Your name indeed, was Chattabhai the Cunning. We
have seen in court as evidence the television advertisement you produced, and a
highly professional and persuasive work it is. And so I have no doubt where one
third of *your* sentence will be spent. Working in an advertising agency of course,
where all your cunning can be employed on parting the public from their money.

For as my old friend Dr Johnson said, 'Men and women are seldom so innocently employed as when they are making money'.

And then Mr Justice Tata turned to the bandit kingpin. 'Javed the Accumulator' he said – 'now *what* is to be done with you?' He paused for effect, and then continued – 'Actually I think it is also quite simple. We have heard that you created loyalty amongst your employees by running an efficient organisation, and seeing that their children were all well-educated. Even though I deplore what your organisation did, I have to admire its efficiency. There is no doubt in my mind' said Mr Justice Tata, 'that you could become a senior executive of a major organization, and so create wealth in our great land. And so one third of your sentence will be spent studying for a business degree, and in the end I hope you will accumulate merit and the respect of your employees rather than gold'.

'And that reminds me', said the judge, 'all this gold must be returned to those from who it was stolen. And so all of you, before you leave, must melt down all this gold again so that all your victims can be compensated. And every child who you robbed of their toys will get a half-sovereign ingot – that is the order of the court'.

Mr Justice Tata always enjoyed saying that, it sounded so good. 'That is the order of the court'. And so off he went to lunch feeling he had done his best, for the victims, for the biscuit bandits themselves, for the children, and for the country.

And as the journalists and the members of the public left the court room they found Oscar the elephant, standing outside with his mahout, with a broad smile on his face. He lifted his trunk and gave his famous war cry that they had heard about in court.

It appeared on the news that evening, but there was no mention of Mani mouse, Uncle Rajan, and Veera, Meera and Kala. But they always knew that without them the case would never have been cracked. And sometimes, when looking at the photo of Javed at the police station, an observant person would ask: 'Why are there five little mice at the front, standing on their hind legs?' And so, in the end, there was some little memorial for all their effort, even though no one had the slightest idea of the story behind it.

For more by John Webster visit
www.johnmwebster.co.uk

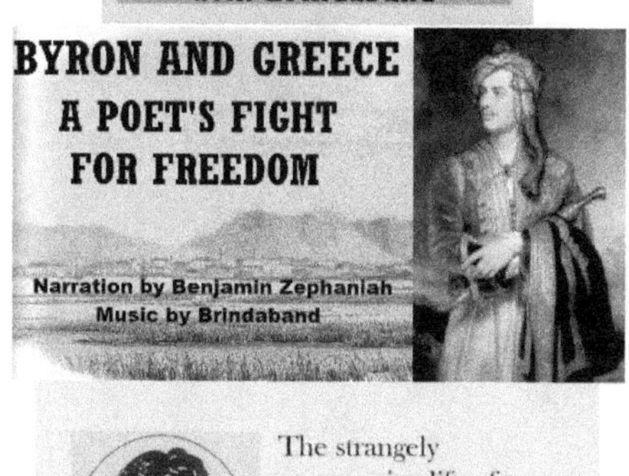

THE
CLOSEST THING
IN HISTORY

THE FAB FOUR

and the

YOUNGER ROMANTICS

JOHN WEBSTER

An entertaining and illuminating comparison of two great cultural forces

www.ingramcontent.com/pod-product-compliance
Lightning Source LLC
Chambersburg PA
CBHW051457050726
47593CB00005B/2112